Saint Benedict

The Man and His Work

by
Adalbert de Vogüé

Translated by
Gerald Malsbary

St. Bede's Publications
Petersham, MA

Originally published in France under the title
Saint Benoît: L'homme et l'oeuvre
©2001 Abbaye de Bellefontaine
collection *Vie Monastique, 40*

PRINTED IN THE UNITED STATES OF AMERICA

LIBRARY OF CONGRESS CATALOGING-IN-PUBLICATION DATA

Vogüé, Adalbert de.
  [Saint Benoît. English]
  Saint Benedict : the man and his work / by Adalbert de
Vogüé; translated by Gerald Malsbary. -- 1st English ed.
    p. cm.
  Includes bibliographical references.
  ISBN 1-879007-48-7
  1. Benedict, Saint, Abbot of Monte Cassino. 2. Chris-
tian saints--Italy--Biography. 3. Benedict, Saint, Abbot of
Monte Cassino. Regula. 4. Monasticism and religious
orders--Rules. I. Title.

BR1720.B45V6413 2006
271'.02--dc22
[B]
                                        2006045508

Published by: St. Bede's Publications
PO Box 545
Petersham, MA 01366

Table of Contents

PART TWO:
THE RULE OF SAINT BENEDICT

Foreword

In a previous work, I sketched the origins of Western monasticism;[1] the present work considers the person and achievements of Saint Benedict, who would come to occupy a central place in the Latin monastic movement. Our documentation on this man is confined to two texts: his biography, written by Pope Gregory the Great at the end of the sixth century, and his Rule, probably composed by Benedict himself at Monte Cassino between 530 and 560 A.D.

Anyone who intends to contemplate the figure of Saint Benedict today and keep to the essentials, is obliged to undertake a commentary on these two works. In both cases, the fundamental task consists in clarifying a) the structure of the works b) the ordering of facts (in the one) and instructions (in the other) and c) the intentions of the hagiographer and lawgiver, respectively. Such things cannot be discerned without paying attention to the literary design of the work in question. In composing his Life of Saint Benedict, Gregory the Great had in mind not only the facts and achievements narrated to him by the four disciples of the Saint to whom he refers in his exordium, but also a certain type of a "man of God" which he derived from the Bible, from Christian hagiography, and from the history of monasticism. And for his part, while composing his Rule, Benedict ceaselessly recalled Holy Scripture, of which his memory was so full, as well as the monastic legislation that had preceded him, starting with the legislation of the "Master" (*Regula Magistri*) the anonymous author whom Benedict followed step by step at first, and then never ceased to keep in mind even while reinterpreting him more freely.

The present work is intended to guide the reader in an analysis of these two works — the Life of Saint Benedict and his Rule. An austere labor, to be sure, and in no way resembling those agreeable narrations that "Lives of Saints" normally strive to provide; yet such a study can lead to a truer and more profound grasp of the subject. For my part, I will not attempt to replace the Second Book of the Gregorian *Dialogues* with a biography in the modern style, nor replace the Rule of Saint Benedict with a personal impression of Benedictine monasticism. Supposing that a reader has already read the works of Gregory and Benedict, we offer instead the opportunity of a new reading, calling attention to certain facts and relationships that may not have appeared at first. Afterwards, there would be nothing better for such a reader to do than go back and look again at the Saint's biography and Rule — with new eyes.

[1] A. de Vogüé, le Monachisme en Occident avant saint Benoît (Vie Monastique, 35), Bellefontaine, 1998.

PART ONE

THE LIFE OF SAINT BENEDICT

Chapter One

The *Dialogues* of Gregory the Great

The life of Saint Benedict lies at the heart of the *Dialogues*, a vast hagiographic masterpiece written by Pope Gregory I, also known as Gregory the Great.

The figure of Benedict within the Dialogues

Written near the beginning of Gregory's pontificate in the years 593-594, the *Dialogues* give the impression of a triptych crowned with an upper panel. The triptych, comprising the first three books, is covered with a multitude of saintly figures and miraculous scenes, nearly all of sixth century Italy. The fourth and last book is oriented toward the world to come, while continuing to speak of further marvelous events here below in the same period and region. Longer than the foregoing books, it treats of the Last Things: death, heaven, and hell, and concludes with an urgent plea for the celebration of the Eucharist, the sure means given for our salvation.

Saint Benedict occupies an enormous and central position within this hagiographical triptych and its surmounting eschatological panel. For not only does his biography (with its thirty miracles) take up the central part of the triptych (Book II), but the eschatological epilogue (Book IV) is introduced by an account of Benedict's death and the ascension of his soul to heaven. Amid the fifty-some figures of minor saints who teem over the two "side panels" (Books I and III) and amid the multitude of similar figures that appear across the "upper panel" (Book IV), the great wonder worker of Subiaco and Monte Cassino strides like a giant.

The dominant personality of sixth century Italy in the realm of grace and sanctity, this "Blessed One" (*Benedictus*) of

Nursia was without a doubt the consummate expression of the biographer's own ideals. In this young man who was able to leave the world so early in life for the service of God, the writer recognized a model he was sorry *not* to have imitated himself, since Gregory had long postponed his own renunciation of the world and entrance into God's service. Those three years of absolute self-effacement that Benedict spent in the grotto of Subiaco, and especially his return to the same spot "to live with himself under God's observing eye alone", were a translation into action of the profoundest longings of the contemplation-loving monk that Gregory himself had become. Furthermore, Benedict's tranquil acceptance of the directive responsibilities imposed upon him set an example for the Bishop of Rome, a frustrated contemplative whose sorrow can be felt from the very beginning of the *Dialogues*.

From Martin to Benedict:
Gregory and Sulpicius Severus

To return to the structure of the work itself and the position occupied by Benedict within it, it is interesting to compare this Gregorian work with the earlier hagiographic achievement after which it was modeled: the writings of Sulpicius Severus on Saint Martin of Tours and the monks of Egypt. More than two centuries before Gregory composed the *Dialogues*, a man of letters from southern Gaul, Sulpicius Severus of Aquitaine, had celebrated in writing the great monk-bishop of Tours, who, thanks to this very writer, would become the leading holy monk of the West. Martin was still living in 396 when Sulpicius sketched out his life, a biography graced by over twenty miracles.

After the biography was rounded out with a supplement of three letters — written the following year to recount the death and funeral of the saintly bishop—this initial work was followed seven years later by a new collection, appropriately entitled the *Dialogues*, which Sulpicius began with the narrative of his friend Postumianus, recently returned from Egypt. Postumianus told of his meetings with Egyptian anchorites and monks. Next, the author and his friends exchanged personal memories of Martin. In this way, a second life of Martin was composed, presupposing the first one and complementing it in a very different style: a carefully narrated biography in classical style is followed by an assortment of varied reminiscences, called forth freely by the ebb and flow of conversation.

And so, long before Gregory, Sulpicius had written hagiographic *Dialogues*, and also like him had composed a kind of triptych: two lives of Martin framing the tale of a journey to Egypt that passed in review a number of lesser monastic personalities. Indeed, it has been pointed out that this work of Sulpicius was at one and the same time both an anticipation of Gregory's work and its opposite: like Gregory's *Dialogues,* it brings together into one three-part work the great figure of a Saint and a host of minor heroes; unlike Gregory's work, the Life of Martin is not at the center of the triptych where Benedict will be, but takes up the two "side wings".

Gregory certainly knew the work of his predecessor, whom he discreetly evokes when reporting that the oratory at Monte Cassino had been dedicated to the "Blessed Martin", the forerunner of Benedict in the mission to pagan peasants. Nor was the precedent of Sulpicius Severus' *Dialogues* without influence on the Pope's choice of this particular literary genre for the celebration of Italian saints. Indeed, the entire *oeuvre* of the writer from Aquitaine could have suggested the construction of a hagiographic trilogy combining the celebration of a principal subject with a multitude of secondary figures, even though the relation between these two elements would be inverted in the Roman work, and a vast appendix relating to the afterlife (this without any precedent in Sulpicius) would expand the section of shorter narratives.

From the Homilies of Gregory to his Dialogues

And yet the literary model for our *Dialogues* is not only to be found in this great collection composed two centuries earlier in the south of Gaul. No more than three years earlier, in his *Homilies on the Gospels*, Gregory himself had laid the foundations for his great narrative work. A dozen of these forty homilies contain (normally at the end) one or two edifying tales, usually concerning the dead who have been visibly cursed or blessed, and a good number of these stories are repeated or retold in the last book of the *Dialogues*. And so, while the *Dialogues'* initial triptych is inspired by the Severan model, the final segment on the afterlife draws on the rich vein of eschatological lore that already runs in the homilies delivered to the people of Rome.

Gregory's conversation-partner: Peter the Deacon.

To complete this survey of the *Dialogues,* we need finally direct our attention to two men we meet there: Pope Gregory and Deacon Peter. Beginning with the latter, we note that the collection of Gregory's Letters allows us to follow his career. Beginning as Subdeacon of the Roman church, in his capacity as rector of the patrimony, he was put in charge of the management of the Holy See's estates in Campania and Sicily. Returning to Rome in July 593, at the very moment when Gregory was starting to write the *Dialogues,* he received the Diaconate. Further letters of the Pope give evidence of his subsequent activities.

Blessed with certain administrative talents, Peter the Deacon was also a religious man, and a friend of Gregory's since their early youth, as the Preface of the *Dialogues* informs us. If the "Oh's" and "Ah's" he says in response to the Pope's speeches have a naive and humorous effect, his pertinent remarks and his apt questions often reveal someone with an educated mind, who knows the Scriptures well and contributes effectively to the development of the spiritual themes. Of course, the *Dialogues* are not in the least a kind of "transcript" of an actual conversation; nevertheless, even if the conversation between Gregory and the Deacon Peter can be regarded as a fiction as a whole or in part, in order for the fiction to be a likely one, it supposes that the author has an interlocutor capable of conversing with him on the rather high level on which he has been placed by his papal office.

The Dialogues as the History of a Soul

Such being his partner, what can we say about Gregory himself? His *Dialogues* are not merely a collection of edifying stories that dramatize holy men. The author also reveals himself in many ways. In saying this, we do not refer only to this or that story where Gregory appears as a dramatic character, as in Book III, where he is unable to fast and is cured by the prayer of Abbot Eleutherius, or as in Book IV, where we see his treatment (at once harsh and merciful) of a monk on the Caelian who had died in a state of sin. Beyond these particular narrations where he simply plays a role, Gregory shows himself more broadly and profoundly in many key passages of the work.

The *Dialogues* as a whole are in effect a "Story of a Soul", where we see someone in a state of crisis finding a way toward solutions that can bring comfort. The crisis is described first in the prologue: Gregory shows himself saddened and beleaguered by the crowds of lay people his pastoral duty requires him to face; he misses the life of contemplation he led not long before in his monastery, and his sadness is only renewed as he thinks of the saints who have abandoned themselves to such a life. The mention he makes of these saints while speaking with Deacon Peter leads the latter to ask him for the stories of the miracles, and these will form the very texture of the work.

After the Pope has complied with the Deacon's request by evoking the fifty-some wonder-workers who inhabit the first three books, at the beginning of the fourth book he takes up again the same complaint but in a new fashion. Without taking up his personal issues, this time Gregory describes the universal drama of humanity as a whole, deprived of the joys of paradise by original sin and incapable of even imagining the happiness that was lost by their first ancestor. Nevertheless, the return to paradise has now become possible by Christ and His Spirit. Enlightened by this Spirit, the saints are the witnesses of the invisible world toward which we may direct ourselves.

The last book of the *Dialogues* is wholly intended to strengthen the faith of Christians in the afterlife. The hope for this future life was at the center of Gregory's contemplation when he was a monk, and he tries now with every means at his disposal to stir up the thought of it, and to enkindle desire for it. At the end, he proposes resolutions, centered on the celebration of the Eucharist. The sacrifice of the mass, which allows us, so to speak, to touch the invisible, should be celebrated as often as possible — that is to say, once every day — and it ought to be accompanied by the actions that it calls forth: after it, by a continuous effort of meditation, and before it, by the pardoning of all offenses.

In this impersonal way, then, Gregory then takes up at the end of the *Dialogues* a series of resolutions that will remedy the distress of which he complains in the prologue. A frustrated contemplative, condemned to a priestly activity all too involved in the world, he has at least been blessed—precisely because he is a priest—in the privilege of consecrating the Eucharist, where he finds everything that had been taken away from him. The supreme priesthood, and its pastoral responsibilities that weigh upon him so heavily, has nevertheless given him this incomparable consolation, which he wants to exploit to the full in recovering "paradise lost".

Chapter Two

The Life of Benedict:
The Second Book of the *Dialogues*

Saint Benedict's career: an overview

Let us now proceed to the life of St. Benedict at the center of the Dialogues. It is composed of two unequal parts. In a first phase, the young saint leaves Rome and takes up his residence at Subiaco, where, after spending three years in a grotto, he founds and directs a dozen little monasteries. Afterwards, he moves from Subiaco to Monte Cassino, where he remains until his death. The first phase is brief, in the literary sense: it only occupies the first eight chapters of the book, while the second, "Cassinian" period fills the next thirty. Making allowance for the varying length of the chapters, one could say that Gregory spends twice as much time on the second phase as on the first.

To this quantitative difference must be added a profoundly moral one. While the Subiaco period is punctuated by spiritual tests that endanger the soul of the saint and reveal his virtues, the period after is characterized by a continuous and peaceful radiance: once he has moved into Monte Cassino, Saint Benedict performs only miracles—some of prophecy, some of power—without appearing to undergo any further temptations.

Nevertheless, these two dozen miracles at Monte Cassino conclude in a kind of "fast forward". The last of the twelve miracles of power is not performed by Benedict himself but—against his will—by his sister, the nun Scholastica, who is shown to be more powerful with God than he is, since she has loved

God more. This final reproof of the wonder-worker is followed by a first vision, that of his sister's soul as it mounts to heaven. Gregory then recounts and comments magnificently on a second vision of a soul being brought to heaven, but accompanied by another wondrous sight: as he witnesses the assumption of a dead bishop, Benedict also sees the whole universe gathered within a single ray of divine light.

And thus the Abbot of Monte Cassino progresses from miracles to visions of the next world. And after these, there is nothing left for him but to enter into that same blessed eternity. Duly announced by himself, his death was worthy of the fighter he always was: he dies in the monastery's oratory, standing in prayer, and held up by his sons. After two of these sons have received a vision of his journey to heaven, the narration returns at last to Subiaco, where an isolated, posthumous miracle takes place in the very grotto that had sheltered the young hermit at the beginning of his career.

The chronology of Benedict's life

The framework of the biography is therefore rather simple, and one would like to pinpoint exactly the dates of the principal events. However, chronological order is the least of our biographer's concerns. He never says at what age Benedict accomplished this or that, nor does he furnish any date of general historical background. But Gregory does provide us with a very useful indication in the prologue: he says that his account is based on the witness of four monks, personal disciples of the saint, whom he has interviewed in person. This means that the chronological gap between the narrator and his hero is not very great. Benedict had to have lived up to the middle of the sixth century, in the last decade of which Gregory wrote the *Dialogues*.

This general dating is corroborated and made more precise by two particular episodes from the Cassinian period, which can be connected with facts otherwise known. First, there is the solemn visit paid to Monte Cassino by the Gothic king Totila, preceded by three of his Counts, a visit that occasioned two of Benedict's "cognitive" miracles. The encounter would appear to have taken place in the second half of 546: certainly before 552 (the year of Totila's death) and, to be precise, before December 546 (the death date of one of the Counts).

The other well-known date is the death of Bishop Germanus of Capua, an event which Benedict saw in a vision. Since Germanus's successor Bishop Victor was consecrated on February 23, 541, Germanus must have died toward the end of 540, perhaps, as local tradition maintains, on October 3.

By 546 Benedict was a renowned personality, as is proven by Totlila's visit to him. One would then be inclined to think that he was a man of rather advanced age at that time. However, the "traditional" dating of his death to 547 does not agree very well with certain admitted facts concerning his Rule, which does not appear to have been completed before the decade 550-560. At the other end of the saint's existence, the currently accepted date of his birth (480) can be postponed another ten years as well.

In any event, of course, the only certainly measured portion of this life is the initial period of three years spent in the grotto of Subiaco. As for the two great phases, situated respectively at Subiaco and Monte Cassino, we do not know the year when the first ended and the second began. The received date of 529 is not unlikely, but is not based on any certain fact, nor even, as far as we know, on any otherwise significant clue.

The saint's spiritual itinerary

We have said enough now to satisfy, at least in summary fashion, the legitimate curiosity of the modern reader, who is accustomed to admire historical figures whose spatial, chronological, social and political coordinates have been indicated as precisely as possible. But if we really hope to profit from the Second Book of the *Dialogues*, we must attend to other objects. What matters is not to reconstruct the career of the man Benedict, by using what little his biographer did tell us and adding to it what conjecture from other sources or our own common sense can tell us about what the biographer *did not* tell us, but rather to enter into the design of the hagiographer, to expound his vision of the life of the saint: to understand from within, in the light of the Scriptures he so often cites, the spiritual trajectory he wants to describe.

What, then, is the itinerary that the Life of Benedict traces? It is that of a young Christian of well-to-do family, whom his parents of Nursia, north of Rome, sent to the capital city for education and preparation for a secular career, but who, instead, took offense at the excessively liberal morality of the student environment, and decided to leave Rome with the intention of consecrating his life to the service of God.

I. The Monk of Subiaco

When breaking with the intention of his parents, the young man did not seem to take the trouble to secure their agreement or even tell them. His break was radical: a break not only from the world, but also from those who sent him into the world. Nevertheless, while leaving for the mountains east of Rome, he still kept one connection with his family: his nurse, who still lived with him at Rome, accompanied him on this first stage of his journey. At once servant and mother, she is the first feminine figure of a story in which women intervene many times, and sometimes decisively.

Rejection of vainglory, radiance toward his neighbors

Without intending to, his nurse would provoke one of those sudden and profound changes that punctuate Benedict's life. Journeying east of Rome, the young man and his companion stopped at the village of Enfide (today, Affile) about sixty kilometers from the City, where they subsisted on the charity of some well-to-do Christians. The nurse had borrowed a sieve to sift wheat with, but it fell off a table and broke in two. The tears of the devastated woman moved Benedict, who prayed and obtained the miraculous repair of the broken utensil. But the general admiration that this first miracle caused brought about a strange and radical reaction in him: in order to avoid the veneration of the inhabitants of Enfide, he left the village in secret, without even saying goodbye to his nurse, and headed toward Subiaco, a little to the north, where he hoped to disappear from everyone's sight in the wilderness.

With the help of Romanus, a monk he found there, Benedict installed himself in a grotto where he would live alone for three years, unknown to anybody. Romanus, the only one aware of him, looked out for his survival by hoisting up to him by rope some bread that had been secretly set aside for his rations. Down the hill from the grotto was the monastery where Romanus lived, governed by a certain abbot named Adeodatus. Without telling his abbot, then, this community-living monk [or "cenobite", from the Greek *koinos bios*, "common life"] was assuring the subsistence of a solitary hermit, whom he had also supplied with a monk's habit.

This nearly complete disappearance of Benedict would come to an end, after three years had passed, thanks to two encounters contrived by Providence. First, a priest in the vicinity received a revelation that Benedict was there, and a command to bring him an Easter meal. Next, the shepherds discovered him, and after mistaking him for a wild animal, became aware of his saintliness. A fair exchange is established: they support him with food, he provides them with good counsel.

We can stop there. These few events already form a complete cycle, which we must observe and understand before going any further. In fact, this same cycle will be repeated several times. It is composed of three phases: first, a temptation; second, a heroic response; finally, an emanation or flashing-forth of sanctity.

The first temptation, which we have just witnessed, was that of vainglory: the young miracle worker from Affile had felt a cloud of incense growing around him, which threatened to go to his head. He reacted heroically to this temptation of pride or vanity, by withdrawing himself from all human observation. In an unexpected way, this radical reaction then enabled him to bring light to his neighbor. Though modest and limited, his influence was none the less already spiritual: many of these shepherds who mistook him for a beast were "drawn away from their bestial mentality" by him and were "led to the grace of piety".

Rejection of sex; spiritual fertility

However, this first emanation engendered another trial. This time, the temptation is expressly attributed to the Tempter par excellence, namely, the devil. This very personage had already attempted to cut off supplies to the young hermit by breaking the little bell that Romanus used to announce his shipments of food. This time, he takes the shape of an annoying blackbird flying about Benedict's face. Chased away by the sign of the cross, the blackbird is followed by a severely carnal temptation: the memory of a woman he had seen throws Benedict into confusion. Doubtless this was one of those folk of modest circumstances who had come to visit him in his grotto.

The second cycle of temptation is enmeshed with the first: the effulgence that followed his victory over vainglory occasions a new temptation – this time, of sex. Benedict reacts to this wave of carnal concupiscence by a new heroic act: he rolls, naked, in thorns and nettles. The sexual desire subsides immediately. The young hermit who was already dreaming of re-entering the world, will remain in his solitude, at God's service. Moreover, he will now shine forth with a new and more profound brightness than before: from now on, people will be leaving the world to put themselves to school with him, to learn the life of perfection from him.

His renunciation of glory won as its fruit the beginning of his religious influence. By the same logic, the renunciation of sexual pleasure brought with it a veritable spiritual fecundity: Benedict begets a people of God in his own image.

Rejection of violence, government of the community

Nevertheless, this new "radiance" leads in turn to a new trial: the temptation of anger and hatred. Benedict's reputation caused him to be elected abbot of a monastery in the neighborhood. Now, this community was not a very good one. When the young superior took steps to reform it, the monks wanted to be rid of him, and tried to poison him.

Miraculously discovered—the poisoned pitcher bursts when blessed by the sign of the cross—the murder attempt put Benedict in the presence of one of those actions that understandably stir up in the targeted person a huge reaction of defensive and vindictive hostility. But the saint reacted otherwise. "His visage remained peaceful, his soul tranquil", and he contented himself with bidding his would-be assassins a gentle adieu.

In this way, we see the perfect control Benedict exercised over what the ancients called the "irascible appetite". The other appetite, the "concupiscible" was already defeated in the temptation of lust. Behind that, in turn, the temptation of vainglory was lying in wait, to come forth to attack the "rational element", the third and highest component of a spiritual being. Thus Benedict will have been tested in turn in each of the three great realms of the moral life: first, the rational, then the concupiscible, and finally the irascible. And this means that his soul was confirmed in mastery of itself and as fully committed to God. The three successive temptations show that he was entirely pure.

This third victory over temptation will end, as the earlier ones, in a new kind of saintly effulgence. Nevertheless it is followed at the outset by a withdrawal into solitude that can already be considered one of its fruits. Returning to his "well-loved solitude" in which he had passed his first three years, Benedict lives there "alone with himself in God's eyes". The beautiful commentary that Gregory adds to these words allows us a glimpse of the contemplative flight of the saint's soul, the natural effect of the integral purification he has been undergoing.

This first result of the failed poisoning is itself soon followed by an influx of monastic vocations who want to place themselves under the direction of the solitary of Subiaco. And so numerous are they, that Benedict distributes them to twelve different monasteries, giving twelve monks to each, while keeping a few with himself. This new glory as master of cenobites surpasses the previous ones in extent and profundity. He begins with teaching the peasants, goes on to direct individual souls in love with perfection, and finally we see him organizing and directing whole communities.

Restraining hatred: the light of the candelabra

First, then, a temptation for some key moral vulnerability; second, a heroically virtuous reaction; third, an ever more profound influence upon those around him: this three-fold dialectic is developed three times, gradually elevating the saint to a kind of summit. But just as each of the first two cycles occasion the subsequent temptations by way of the very glory in which they end, just so too the third one will not remain "closed up" in itself, but will engender a new trial in its turn. Nevertheless, this one will only be a repetition of the preceding: as if the Lord wanted to be assured once again of the saint's dominion over his irascibility, he exposes him to a new attempt at poisoning.

But this time, the murder attempt is the work not of a group but of an individual: the priest of the neighboring parish, Florentius, has taken offense at the renown of this monk, and after a vain attempt to discredit him, decides to get rid of him by poison. In the previous episode, the toxic material was wine. This time, it is bread, which Florentius poisons and sends to Benedict under the pretext of giving him some blessed bread.

In both cases, a miraculous event accompanies the discovery of the hidden trap. The jar of wine was broken under the sign of the cross; now, Benedict intuits (we do not know how) the mortal danger, and commands his trained crow to take the bread off to a deserted place and throw it away.

But these differing details are less important than the profound similarity of the Saint's internal reactions. The tranquility of spirit and countenance with which Benedict received the revelation of the first murder attempt is now succeeded by a no less peaceful reaction, mixed though it is with a certain sadness: "He grieved more for the other priest than for himself".

The temptation to hatred is thus overcome the second time more effectively than the first. A veritable love pours forth in Benedict's compassion for the would-be murderer. Still more precisely, the sudden death of Florentius, which takes place soon after, brings out clearly the charity that fills Benedict's soul: when he receives the news of his enemy's demise, he mourns as if he had lost a dear friend, and he deplores the fact that the disciple who reported the news appeared happy about it.

When Benedict was attacked by the wicked monks, he immediately took his departure. After the criminal attempt of the priest, he did not remove himself from the battlefield. It is only when Florentius endangers the disciples—by making young maidens dance naked under their windows—that Benedict decides to leave the place, in order to stop the persecution.

This departure from Subiaco initiates the last phase of the threefold cycle to which we have grown accustomed: the radiance of glory that follows the victory over temptation. Tempted by hatred, and victorious over it a second time, Benedict will go on to exercise a still greater influence. Since he has been obliged to leave, he will go on to make foundations elsewhere: to the twelve monasteries of the Anio valley he adds that of Cassino. In thus passing from a fortified valley to an elevated location that commands vast territory, the man of God rises to a greater renown. The lamp that was under the bushel appears to have become a candelabra. In fact, as we shall see, the radiance that Benedict will send forth from there will be of a new kind. For the first time, we will see him attacking the remnants of paganism, demolishing idolatrous shrines and preaching the faith.

The miracles of Subiaco and the Bible

But before we join Benedict in leaving Subiaco, we notice that in the course of the last two temptations a series of four miracles has taken place. The first one consisted in seeing an invisible demon and putting him to flight: this evil spirit, who was dragging a monk away from the oratory at prayer time, appeared to his eyes under the appearance of a black infant—we may think of St. Anthony's temptation—and the victim was cured by the blow of a staff. Then, by his prayer, Benedict brought it about that a new spring of water would leap forth from a mountain peak when three of his monasteries were suffering from lack of water. Another time, he recovered an axe from the depths of a lake: the iron axe-head rose up from the bottom and joined itself to the handle that Benedict stretched forth to it. Finally, one of his monks, little Placidus, fell into the lake, and the saint commanded another young disciple, Maurus, to go rescue him. We then see Maurus walk out upon the water, grab the child by the hair and lead him back to the shore.

Each of these marvelous stories contains one or more instructive details, and allow us a glimpse of the monastic life led by Benedict and his monks. But the attention of the narrator is actually pointing in another direction. What interests Gregory is the resemblance of each miracle to a miraculous event in Sacred History: the water leaping from the rock recalls Moses; the iron brought from the lake recalls Eliseus, the walking on water recalls the Apostle Peter. Leaving aside the first marvel—the vision of the devilish imp and his expulsion—the author of the *Dialogues* extends his typological research to two later facts we have mentioned before: the bread carried by the crow at his command recalls Elias, and the tears shed at the death of an enemy makes Benedict resemble David.

In this way a series of five figures is formed recalling five scriptural personages: Moses, Eliseus, Peter, Elias and David.

Although Gregory does not mention it explicitly , the ordering of these five within this gallery is worthy of our attention: in the middle, St. Peter, the only saint mentioned here from the New Testament; at either side of him Elias and Eliseus, the two great prophets of the Old Law; finally, and standing further away, Moses and David, both also more remote in history. This symmetrical arrangement clearly imitates the Roman mosaics of the sixth century, such as that in the Basilica of Saints Cosmas and Damian, where Christ is joined by the two great apostles, by two physician brothers, and finally by two more recent personages, symmetrically placed on either side.

Nevertheless, we should not forget that all of these miracles are accomplished by a single wonder-worker: St. Benedict the Monk. After connecting each one of them to its Biblical model, Peter the Deacon concludes that the Saint of Subiaco was "filled with the Spirit of all the Just". Nothing shows better than this formula the profound design of the author, who celebrates this saint of the century, only to direct the attention of his readers toward Holy Scripture. The Life of Benedict, like the entire *Dialogues* of which it forms the center, is really the Old and New Testament, made present, actualized, and prolonged into the days of Gregory and the Christians for whom he wrote.

II. The Abbot of Monte Cassino

Benedict's installation at Monte Cassino was accompanied by a campaign to evangelize the rural inhabitants, among whom the pagans still outnumbered the Christians. Arriving at the mountain top, the saint found there a "temple of Apollo", as Gregory says (it may have been a temple of Jupiter) along with "sacred groves, dedicated to the service of demons", where "a crowd of infidels were still at that time offering their sacrilegious sacrifices".

The struggle against paganism and demons

Benedict's violent action — he breaks the idol, overturns the altar and razes the sacred trees – recalls not only the imperious destroyers of the Old Testament, but still more the missionary campaigns of Saint Martin in fourth-century Gaul as reported by Sulpicius Severus. We can be certain that the model of the Bishop of Tours was present in Benedict's mind, since he dedicates to St. Martin the oratory that replaces the temple of Apollo, while dedicating a second oratory on the summit of the mountain to St. John the Baptist.

This anti-pagan action by Benedict is a direct offensive on the "prince of this world", the inspiration and object of idolatrous cults. Satan's reaction is immediately translated into embodied images and insults, then by a series of catastrophes: a stone will not budge despite the brothers' attempts to lift it, an illusory fire threatens to engulf the kitchen, a wall collapses and crushes a young monk. On each occasion, Benedict remedies the evil through prayer: the stone is lifted, the apparent fire disappears, the little monk returns to his work, safe and sound.

These first three miracles of Monte Cassino, uniformly obtained by prayer, form a contrast with the five Biblical prodigies of Subiaco, of which only the first (the spring of water from the mountain) resulted from a prayer of the saint. Earlier, to be sure, Benedict had prayed for the repair of the sieve at Affile, and likewise had prayed to see the diabolical tempter of Maurus and Pompeianus, but these events were too isolated from each other in time to produce the same impression as the three brief incidents of the present *section*. In these, Benedict appears decisively as a man of prayer, as one who has recourse to prayer to get to the bottom of all difficulties.

As if to make the lesson all the more striking, Gregory introduces the third event—the healing of the crushed child—

by showing Benedict being visited by the devil during his prayer. Then, he says, the saint ordered the child to be laid out on the mat where he was accustomed to prostrate himself in prayer. When we read, finally, that the Abbot of Cassino "set himself to pray more fervently than he was accustomed to" in order to obtain the recovery of the young monk, the image of Benedict as a man of prayer has at last succeeded in imposing itself upon the mind of the reader.

The "two dozen" miracles

Nevertheless, these three demon episodes are only an introduction to the Cassino period, which comprises no less than twenty-four marvelous deeds, set forth in fine order: twelve "cognitive" miracles, followed by twelve "operative" ones. After having shown Benedict as the prophet who could discern the invisible and foresee the future, Gregory hails him as the Friend of God whose words, gestures, and even mere glances (let alone his prayers) have an unexpected efficacy. Only the last of these dozen miracles of power will not be carried out as he wanted, but will happen against his will, thanks to the superior power of his own sister Scholastica.

These two dozen prodigies that form the center of the Cassinian period are preceded by the three satanic episodes we have just finished with, and will be followed, in symmetrical fashion, by three eschatological visions: we will see, first, the soul of Scholastica mount heavenward, then the soul of Bishop Germanus, and finally that of Benedict himself. Between the three initial encounters with the devil and the three concluding ascensions to God, the deeds and accomplishments of Benedict at Monte Cassino are set forth in a systematic, non-chronological order.

At Subiaco, we may recall, the Saint passed through a series of tests, where each temptation gave rise in its own turn to a new heroic reaction and led him to exercise a new kind of influence upon his neighbor. Without undergoing any further temptations, at Monte Cassino Benedict exerts his charismatic influence quietly in the two forms we have mentioned. After the upward climb of Subiaco, the Cassinian period takes place as a whole upon a single high plateau.

The miracles of prophecy

"In these circumstances, the man of God began to be endowed as well with the spirit of prophecy, announcing the future, and making known to those in his presence what was happening a long distance away." (11,3). These words, by which Gregory introduces the twelve cognitive miracles he is going to relate, distinguish two kinds of effects of the "spirit of prophecy": the prediction of future things, and the announcement of things taking place far way.

In fact, these two types of cognitive miracles will be presented in an opposed order: at first, two deeds of knowing at a distance (12, 13), and then, after a brief interval, four predictions (15-18). Between these two kinds of "prophetic" events, duly announced each in its turn, the third miracle will be of a somewhat different and unexpected kind: Benedict unmasks a fraud, when he recognizes the horseman Riggo behind the appearance of King Totila (14).

The last miracles of the series present the same succession of knowledge at a distance (18-19) or predictions (21-22), separated by an original phenomenon: the seer reads the hidden thoughts in the heart of a monk (20). This time, nevertheless, the first of the predictions is accompanied by knowledge at a distance (18), and the last is paired up with a novel occurrence: the saint shows himself in a dream to two sons of his who are far away, and gives them instructions.

In this aretological framework, which occasions several biblical dissertations — on Paul, Nathan, Elisha, and Habakuk — Gregory shows the man of God in relation to various categories of persons and lets us see the life he leads with his sons at Monte Cassino. Twice we are witnesses to the departure of one or two brothers, sent forth from the monastery on some mission or another. On the occasion of one of these, two monks are sitting down to eat with a pious woman, thus acting contrarily to the Rule, which prohibited any meals outside the monastery. Another time, once a brother had completed the exhortation he was assigned to give to some nuns, he accepted handkerchiefs from them, again a violation of the Rule.

Inside the monastery, one day we see Benedict having dinner at a late hour, which requires him to have a brother monk stand near him with a lighted lamp. This is rather astonishing, because the Benedictine Rule prescribes eating in daylight, no matter what season of the year. Perhaps it was an exceptional circumstance, but this same twist on the Rule will be repeated, as we shall see, during the saint's final meeting with his sister.

In this episode of the evening dinner, the lamp is held by a monk who is the son of a *Defensor*, the title of an important local office. We may note here that Benedict has already welcomed to Subiaco two children of Roman nobility, Maurus and Placidus. At Monte Cassino, other secular persons would appear here and there. Two of them are very significant: a brother of the Monk Valerian goes on foot every year to Monte Cassino, without eating anything during his day-long journey; Theopropus, however, a nobleman from the neighboring town Cassinum, is "converted", that is, consecrated to God within the world, and he is highly esteemed by the saint to whom he owes his conversion. On the other hand, Exhilaratus steals some of the wine that his master had entrusted him to carry to the monastery. Nevertheless, he will "convert" and Gregory gives us to understand that Exhilaratus would eventually join the clergy at Rome.

Of course, we also see Benedict in friendships with members of the clergy. The Bishop Constantius of Aquino, his near neighbor, sends him a cleric who is tormented by the devil, whom Benedict exorcises and advises never to receive any holy orders. Another prelate, Sabinus of Canosa, comes to visit him and talks with him about contemporary events.

Beside these people who appear in the ordinary Roman world, many narratives depict the formidable barbarians by whom Italy was ravaged in the sixth century. Already the cycle of Subiaco had shown a Goth whose surprising humility—he was one of the "poor in spirit"—brought about his entrance to the monastery of the saint. The Goths reappeared shortly, but with very different facial expressions. Their King Totila put the prophetic charism of Benedict to the proof by sending him his squire Riggo, dressed like the sovereign and escorted by three famous counts in the usual entourage of the monarch. Unmasked at first sight by the man of God, the charade was followed by an authentic visit of the king, who then heard Benedict's predictions about the last ten years of his reign and his death.

Around the same period, this prophecy was supplemented by an announcement concerning the fate of Rome. More clairvoyant than his friend the saintly Bishop of Canossa, who believed that Rome would be destroyed by the barbarians, Benedict predicted that the City would gradually dwindle; Gregory could sadly confirm this fifty years later.

The ravages caused by war were doubtless the cause of the famine that ravaged Campania and gave Benedict the occasion to prophesy the coming of divine assistance. Miraculously helped in these circumstances, the monastery at Monte Cassino would nevertheless be destroyed after the passing of the saint, as he in fact discerned in a revelation. But this destruction will be the doing not of the Goths but of the Lombards.

The tears Benedict sheds when he learns of the future annihilation of his work are a moving sign of a humanity similar to our own. That the souls—that is, the lives—of his followers are saved is not enough to restore his serenity. The destruction of the buildings he has erected devastates him.

On the occasion of these tears of suffering love observed by Theopropus, Gregory notes an abiding characteristic of the man of God: he cries while praying, something that he recommends several times in the Rule, as we shall see. The affective intensity of his relationship with God is only equaled by a tranquil detachment in his relationships with the great ones of this world. Neither at the feigned nor at the true visit of the King does he take the trouble to stand up. Finally if he does get up and walk over to Totila, it is only to lift the King up from the ground, who had fallen on his face, petrified by fear.

The last of Benedict's twelve cognitive miracles reveal two further aspects of his life and work: his activity as founder and the nature of the confinement he imposed on himself. A property was offered to him at Terracina, not far from the sea. He sends a group of monks there to set up the new foundation, but never goes there himself. When the time comes to begin building, he gives instructions to the "Father" (or Abbot) and the "Praepositus" (or Prior) one after the other, by appearing in their dreams.

It is clear that Benedict decided he would never leave. In fact, after the first preaching to the peasants of the region, we never do see him leave Monte Cassino. The most he does is to visit his sister every year, who lives a short distance from the monastery, as Gregory will explain in a later passage. But when it comes to real departures, there are none, whether we speak of Subiaco or Monte Cassino. In this respect, the Life of Benedict certainly differs profoundly from the Life of Martin, in which Sulpicius Severus has Martin so frequently "on the road".

The miracles of power

The astounding way of communicating that the saint has just employed in the episode about Terracina — he makes himself understood in a dream to two men as they sleep — provokes a question from Deacon Peter, which in turn sets off a new series of stories: Gregory's interlocutor would like to know how Benedict used ordinary speech. In answer to this question, Gregory immediately pronounces the word that sums up all that follows: *virtus*, or "power": Even Benedict's ordinary speech was powerful, as the stories that follow will show.

After the miracles of prophecy, then, we have the miracles of power. The new series will comprise twelve miraculous events, as did the preceding series, but an accident occurs at its end, so that the twelfth miracle, instead of being the work of the saint, will be carried out by his sister, the nun Scholastica, whose prayer, against Benedict's wishes, will bring about a rainstorm that will compel the two to remain in each other's company for an entire night.

The eleven miracles of power by Benedict himself can be sorted into four smaller groups, in which the beneficiaries of the wonderworker are alternatively monks or secular folk. The first three miracles bring monastic personages to the stage, while the next three concern lay persons. Then once again Benedict works miracles for his own sons three times, before going on to work two more miracles for people on the outside.

Like the stories in the prophetic section, these new tales usually show monks and nuns at fault in some way, for whom the miraculous word of Benedict has an effect either of chastisement for what they deserve or of liberation from the regrettable consequences of their conduct. In this way, to begin with, two nuns who misused their powers of speech and had brought upon themselves an excommunication from the saint, died a few days later, not to rest in peace until Benedict relieved them from excommunication by celebrating the Eucharist. Similarly, a young monk who left the monastery without permission, died suddenly, and his body was rejected by the earth until the moment when Benedict placed a consecrated host on the dead man's chest. These two very similar stories are of interest in showing us the uses made — an especially surprising use in the second case — of the Eucharist in assisting the dead in sixth century Italy.

The last miracle of this first group at one and the same time strikes and saves an apostate monk, who, after having tired Benedict with his complaints, was planning to quit the monastery. The prayer of the saint brings about a vision of the devil, who terrifies the monk and makes him change his mind and re-enter the monastery. Two features of Benedict appear in this incident: his anger and his prayer. This latter will reappear three times in the present section, where the last miracle — the one by Scholastica — will likewise be obtained by prayer. And as regards the anger (*ira*) of the holy abbot, who had grown tired of the demands of that faithless monk, it will resurface, we shall see, on the occasion of the disobedience of one of the monks.

The two deeds that follow share in common the advantage of having particular witnesses, whom Gregory mentions by name: first, a person of high rank, the "illustrious" Aptonius, and second, one of the saint's disciples, a certain Peregrinus. These two occasional narrators can be added to the four abbots cited in the Prologue, to whom Gregory owes all his knowledge of Benedict. As for the miracles in this group, where only secular persons are involved, the first and the third are healings of leprosy, while the second is a money matter, solicited by a debtor who has need of twelve *solidi* of gold — and that is no insignificant sum, for it is the price of a horse. Benedict does not simply find the desired money in his money chest, but brings it about through prayer that Providence sends him (we don't learn how) thirty solidi, to the utmost satisfaction of the debtor.

Telling of the two days of prayer that obtained this last miracle, Gregory notes that praying this way, in an intense and prolonged fashion, was a "habit" of Benedict. This allows us a glimpse of his spiritual physiognomy. In fact, as we have seen, prayer will reappear many times in the course of the Second Book of the *Dialogues*, especially in the miracles of power.

The trilogy of miracles that follows brings us into the interior of the Cassinian community. A famine that ravages Campania — something that was mentioned in the second-to-last miracle of prophecy — causes a shortage of oil. The little that is left at Monte Cassino — at the bottom of a glass flask — is given away by Benedict to a needy subdeacon who has come in search of oil. Now the cellarer of the monastery who received the order to give the bottle to the subdeacon, judges the order as senseless and refuses to carry it out. When Benedict learns of this disobedience, he becomes irritated and has the thing thrown out of the window. Against all expectation, the glass vessel falls upon the rocks but does not break. After making sure the subdeacon gets it, Benedict performs a second miracle by obtaining through his own prayer, in conjunction with the prayer of all the brothers, that an empty jar becomes brimful of oil.

A third miracle is added to these two occurrences, which has no chronological connection with them, but is situated like them within the bosom of the community at Cassino. This time the saint's partner in the miracle is not the monastery cellarer but an elderly monk who is the victim of demonic aggression. By a simple slap on the face, Benedict chases away the demon and heals the possessed monk. The incident is of further interest by providing us a sight of two places at Cassino: a water source, most likely a cistern, where the old monk had gone to draw water, and the oratory to Saint John the Baptist on the summit of the mountain, where Benedict went to pray. If the exorcism itself was accomplished by a simple act, without the saint praying for the possessed—something that provokes a question from Deacon Peter—prayer is no less present in the story, as it is so frequently in the miracles of power.

At the end, two connected narratives portray secular visitors to Monte Cassino: first, a ferocious Goth by the name of Zalla, who is dragging in tow some unlucky peasant he wants to rob of a sum of money, and second, a tearful father of a family, bearing his dead son in his arms. Benedict frees the captive peasant and revives the dead child. The first of these two miracles is accomplished by a simple "look" of the Saint which terrifies the Goth and makes the bonds fall from his prisoner, while the resurrection requires ardent prayer which Benedict performs in the manner of Elisha by lying over the body of the dead child. And thus Gregory replies to the question of his deacon which had provoked the two stories: did the Man of God "always obtain his miracles through prayer or did he sometimes achieve them simply by an act of the will?"

These last stories recall earlier ones. Zalla the Goth leads us back to Benedict's interviews with King Totila and his squire, whereas the resurrection of the child reproduces in much more spectacular and dramatic manner one of the first prodigies of Cassinian glory: the holy abbot had restored a little monk to his work in perfect health after he had been crushed to pieces by a falling wall.

The second to last miracle thus recalls the deeds of prophecy, and the last one recalls the struggle with satan at the beginning of the Cassinian period. This double inclusion has the effect of emphasizing that we have reached an end: from now on, Benedict will not act on this earth but will turn toward the hereafter. The twelfth miracle of power will not be accomplished by him but by his sister, in the expectation that she will precede him to heaven and the grave.

Now while these two stories resemble earlier events, they also each show a new aspect of our hero. When Zalla and the peasant arrive at Cassino, Benedict was not only "seated", as he was at the arrival of Riggo and Totila, but furthermore, Gregory notes that he was "reading", something we have not seen him do before. This abbot who sits and reads at the gate of his monastery is a unique spectacle, perhaps necessitated by the story itself.

As for the encounter of Benedict with the other peasant, the one who is carrying his dead child, it takes place the moment when the abbot "was returning from working in the fields with the brothers". We are reminded here of the Benedictine Rule, which states that the monks are obliged to do their own farm work and encourages them to do so, in contrast with the Rule of the Master, which prohibited such work.

The last of the miracles and the first of the visions

The last miracle of power does not have Benedict as its author but his sister Scholastica who obtains her prayer against the wishes of the saint. Soon afterwards Scholastica dies, more saintly than her saintly brother, and enters heaven visibly in the form of a dove. Scholastica is then in turn the accomplisher of the last miracle and the object of the first vision. Putting an end to the operative marvels of Benedict, and providing him with the spectacle of her own entrance into heaven, she causes him to pass from action to contemplation, anticipating that he himself would follow after her, into the beyond.

The two successive stories that make up this pivotal passage have a rare charm. First, we are present at the annual meeting of sister and brother. She, consecrated to God from childhood, travels to visit Benedict every year. The meeting takes place in a dependency of the monastery, a small distance away. After passing a day praising God and talking about Him, the brother and sister dine together at nightfall (Gregory, who already presented Benedict once as dining by the light of a candle, does not seem aware that the Rule prescribes eating in broad daylight only). Not satisfied with this long conversation, Scholastica asks her brother to keep talking with her all night long, to stay until daybreak discussing "the joys of the heavenly life". "Impossible!" Benedict replies, saying he must spend the night in his monastery. Ignoring this refusal, Scholastica begins to pray, and obtains through her tears a torrential downpour which prevents the saint and his companions from returning home. Thus vanquished by his sister and forced to stay where he is, Benedict passes the night with her: "They speak to each other of the spiritual life to their heart's content".

In this victory of the sister over the brother Gregory sees an effect of the greater love that filled the woman: "God is love" (1 John 4, 16), and, the more one loves, the more influence one has on God's heart. *Plus potuit, quae amplius amavit*: in writing this phrase at the conclusion, the author of the *Dialogues* is evidently thinking of Jesus' judgment in favor of the sinful woman at the house of Simon the Pharisee (Luke 7, 47). Scholastica was no public sinner, nor is Benedict in any way a Pharisee, but just as the woman in the Gospel showed more love than Simon, in the same way Benedict's sister on this occasion has shown herself more loving than her brother, bound though he is by the noble concern not to violate the Rule.

This curious and delightful story is followed by a brief account of Scholastica's death. Three days after their last encounter, Benedict sees the soul of his sister ascending to heaven in the form of a dove. He sends for her body and lays it in the tomb he had prepared for himself. Once again, Gregory has a biblical event in mind when he writes that the sister and brother "after having always been spiritually united in God, were no longer separate bodily in the tomb", he is thinking, evidently, of Saul and Jonathan, celebrated by David at their death in like terms (2 Samuel 1,23).

The second vision and final portrait

With this first account of a vision, the author of the *Dialogues* has embarked on the last part of the Life of Benedict, to which nothing is lacking now but one more vision of a soul ascending to heaven and the saint's own entrance into heaven at his death.

The holy soul whose ascension Benedict witnesses is that of Bishop Germanus of Capua, who appears to have died around 540 A.D. Taking place as it did before the visit of King Totila, the death of Germanus is not narrated here according to chronological order, but by reason of the resemblance that his entrance into heaven bears to the ascension of Scholastica (which precedes it) and of Benedict himself (which follows it).

No page of the *Dialogues,* Book II (or even of the work as a whole) is as beautiful as this vision, where Benedict is not only present at the glorification of the soul of a holy Bishop but also beholds the entire universe arrayed before his eyes in a beam of divine light. "To the soul who sees the Creator, the whole creation is small". Now this tininess of the created world that Benedict sees corporally toward the end of his existence in a magnificent vision, he had already seen in spirit long before, when as a youth he was leaving the world to give himself to God. The end of the second book of the *Dialogues* thus corresponds to its beginning, and the initial choice of the young monk is verified at last by a kind of visual perception of the distance between the creator and the creature.

At the level of historical detail, the episode offers the additional interest of bringing to the stage a certain Servandus, whose monastery, founded by the famous patrician Liberius, is supposed to be at or near Naples, i.e. not at Alatri, as the medieval legend holds. This Servandus was a deacon, we are informed—the sole mention in the *Dialogues* of a clerical order being combined with the abbatial office.

No less interesting is the topographical precision Gregory supplies: the abbot of Monte Cassino lodges his guest on the ground-floor of a tower, of which he occupies the upper floor. This abbatial lodging, separated from the dormitory of the monks, and contrary to the prescription of the Rule of the Master, allows us to see in Benedict a tendency to solitude that recalls the first three years of Subiaco. Gregory then presents the saint as "anticipating the time of night prayer" and as devoting himself to private vigils "while the brothers are still sleeping". In this setting and while thus engaged in ascetical practice, Benedict is blessed with his grand cosmic vision.

We also come across the name Theopropus in this passage, the notable resident of Cassino whom Benedict asked to have a message sent to Capua to verify the passing of Bishop Germanus. This pious layman had already been witness to the tears of the saint when the latter announced the future destruction of the monastery at the hands of the Lombards.

Provided with a magnificent commentary, this vision of the hereafter marks at once the summit of Benedict's life and the end of his biography "here below". But before proceeding to the actual departure, Gregory renders homage to the teaching of the great abbot, now consigned to the Rule for Monks that he had written. Praised for the "discernment" that it shows as well as for its literary quality, this work dispenses the biographer from having to trace out a moral portrait of the saint, since he "never taught otherwise than how he lived". At little cost, therefore, Gregory is able to satisfy the obligation that is imposed on every biographer, that of making known the spiritual physiognomy of his hero. This reference to the Benedictine Rule is therefore in one sense "an escape" that deprives us of a portrait we desire, but in another sense provides a precise indication of the actual written work of the saint, a kind of "advertisement" that would contribute powerfully to its diffusion.

Like Benedict's cosmic vision, his "doctrine"—described as "luminous"—should be compared to its austere beginnings. In quitting Rome with his nurse, the young man not only turned his back on the world, he also renounced the worldly learning he had been sent to acquire in the city. "Knowingly ignorant and wisely lacking knowledge" at the time, he is now, no less for all that, a true teacher. Just as his final vision of the universe was a compensation for his initial renunciation of the world, so now his "teaching" is paradoxically the crown of a life devoted to "ignorance".

Death and posthumous miracles

The epilogue of this holy life provides several marvelous events that recall the preceding pages. Just as Benedict's Cassinian period contained twelve miracles of prophecy as well as twelve miracles of power, so his death becomes the object of a last prophecy, and the moments after his death are marked by healings that took place in the grotto of Subiaco, in particular the healing of a madwoman. Between these two series of great events, the death of the saint occurs, in company with a vision granted to two of his sons. Thus—taking into account a certain change of order, since the visions do not follow the prophecies and the works of power, but are inserted between these—we find once again in these last pages the three types of miracles that Gregory admired in the Monte Cassino narrative.

Benedict's prophetic charism manifests itself several times as he approaches his death. This year, he announced to some of his disciples his approaching end as well as the signs that would accompany it. He has his tomb opened six days before, and one day before he dies, has himself brought to the monastery's oratory, where he dies after receiving communion, standing up in prayer and supported by the brothers. This death during prayer recalls the prayer of Paul the first hermit as narrated by St. Jerome. We may also think of the passing of the Emperor Vespasian (born like Benedict at Nursia) who likewise wished to die standing up, as well as the death of a certain abbot Spes whose monastery was near Nursia, and who, according to the fourth book of the *Dialogues*, departed this world the way Benedict did: standing amidst his brothers in the act of praying, after receiving communion.

The ascension of Benedict's soul to heaven clearly recalls those of his sister Scholastica and of Bishop Germanus but this time we see neither dove nor globe of fire. The two brothers who were granted the vision only perceive "a pathway strewn with carpets and shining with countless lamps" and then an angel who lets them know that Benedict has ascended to heaven upon that path. *Ab eius cella in caelum usque*: he has passed from his cell (the monastery) all the way to heaven.

Dying, it seems in the oratory of St. Martin, apparently, Benedict was interred in the oratory of St. John the Baptist at the top of the hill. This topographical precision recalls in turn the saint's first arrival at Monte Cassino and his first labors. Going back further, the posthumous miracles Gregory chooses to report evoke the sojourn of the young man in the grotto of Subiaco. In this way, the successive phases of this holy life are found recapitulated, as it were *in extremis*, at beginning and end, by a series of inclusions.

But this literary design, if design it is, is not of the greatest importance to the narrator. What interests him above all in the return to the grotto at Subiaco is the paradox constituted by the miracles accomplished by Benedict so far distant from his tomb and relics. A lovely disquisition attempts to explain this surprising fact, which would seem to develop the faith of Christians by making them go beyond tangible objects and spatial proximity. Paraphrasing the words of the Christ: " If I do not go, the Paraclete will not come" (John 16, 7) Gregory opposes "corporeal vision" to "spiritual love". *Spiritaliter amare:* these two words, which close both this section and the entire book, speak well of the profound desire of a mystical biographer, who is a historian only for the purpose of leading the souls of his readers to an invisible encounter with the divine.

While letting himself be guided by these intuitions of the spiritual theologian, Gregory is not perhaps inattentive to the fact that the last miracle of Benedict that he tells has for its beneficiary a poor woman. This deranged person, who recovers her reason after a night passed by chance in the grotto of Subiaco, leads us to think of another woman: the nurse who had followed the young world-renouncer all the way to the town of Affile, and whom he had left behind to hide himself at Subiaco. It was on behalf of this servant and mother figure that Benedict—like Christ at Cana—had performed his first miracle, and it is likewise for the benefit of a woman that the last miracle reported by the hagiographer was accomplished. Between these two feminine figures that frame the entire biography, several other women have passed by on the stage, the principal ones being the anonymous person whose seduction almost made him abandon his solitude and the holy Scholastica, who showed herself more loving than he.

But let us not get overly absorbed in such details, and look rather to the design of the hagiographer, which is to leave his reader in the presence of the Christ, corporally invisible, but the object of a spiritual love infused by the Paraclete. The Life of Benedict is the life of a saint, and has no other end than to lead us to sanctity.

PART II:

THE RULE OF SAINT BENEDICT

Chapter One
Introduction:
The Master and Benedict

Gregory attributes a "Rule for Monks" to the hero of the second book of his *Dialogues* and all he says about it is that it is "noteworthy for its discernment and brilliant in its language". Without any doubt this is the monastic Rule said to be written by Benedict, copied in countless manuscripts over the course of the centuries. This is the text we must examine now, if, as Gregory suggests, we want to have an idea of the moral physiognomy of the saint.

Nevertheless, this approach to the person by way of his work requires a minimum of familiarity with the literary genre of the work and with the sources used by the author. What then *is* a "Rule for Monks"? The most primitive monastic legislative texts — of Pachomius, Basil, Augustine, and, we might add, Cassian's *Institutes,* thrown in for good measure — received various names from their authors or translators, but beginning with the first regulations of Lerins — the so-called "Rule of the Four Fathers" and the "Second Rule" — we note a tendency to use the term *regula* for the normative text, always very brief, that governs the monastic community. Five of these short writings, produced by the Lerinian monasticism and its offshoots, form a line that stretches from the beginning of the fifth century to the first third of the sixth.

To this family of Gallic Rules which Caesarius and Aurelian of Arles will soon continue, belongs another line as well, with a different geographical position and format. It is in Italy, not far from Rome, where there seems to have been born in the first quarter of the sixth century the enormous *Regula Magistri*, almost twenty times longer than the "Rule of the Four Fathers". Without treating at length this strange and powerful work (a summary of which can be found in the preceding volume of this series[1]) we will limit ourselves here to reporting that the book has two sequels: around 530, the Neapolitan Eugippius took about fifty of its chapters for his own patchwork Rule. A short time after, Benedict began copying out the entire spiritual portion with only slight modification and abridgement, but then proceeded to adapt the institutional chapters in a much more independent way.

While Benedict's Rule is only a third as long as the *Regula Magistri*, it ought to be read in conjunction with its source text, which can clarify both its origin and meaning. In fact, it is before the background of the Master that we can best discern the intentions and choices of Monte Cassino's founder. This fundamental relationship between the Benedictine Rule and the Rule of the Master is played out in three phases as it were: in its prologue and first seven chapters (*RB Prologue, 1-7*) we shall see how Benedict reproduces his model, at once literally and freely; in the next part (*RB* 8-66), we will follow the course of his reworking and adaptation; finally, in the last chapters (*RB* 67-73), we shall witness the new author's complete emancipation from his model.

---

[1] A. de Vogüé, *le Monachisme en Occident avant saint Benoît* (*Vie Monastique,* 35), Bellefontaine, 1998.

Chapter Two

The Spiritual Part

The Rule of the Master began with a solemn presentation of the three pillars of cenobitism or community spiritual life: the rule, the monastery, and the abbot. Joined together in the definition of cenobites at the beginning of the first chapter, these three fundamental realities became the object of three successive expositions: first, a prologue introduced the Rule itself; second, a vast three-part dissertation (parable of the fountain, commentary on the Lord's Prayer, paraphrase of two psalms) presented the *monastery*, also to be known as the "School of the Lord's Service"; and finally, the long first chapter on the various kinds of monks concluded with an exposition of the *abbot*, considered as a "teacher" accredited by God, and speaking in His name at the monastery, a counterpart to the bishop in the Church.

Benedict and the introductions of the Master

Of these three presentations made by the Master, Benedict formally retains only the second one concerning the monastery, including the title "School of the Lord's Service". The decision to "found" this school, as the Master put it, is reproduced along with the entire paraphrase of the thirty-fourth and fifteenth Psalms that preceded it, while the parable of the fountain completely disappears and the commentary on the Lord's Prayer is barely represented at all, by a brief invitation to prayer (Prologue, 3).

What has become, then, of the other two presentations — of the Rule and abbot? They have both disappeared, so that Benedict's definition of cenobites at the beginning of his first chapter remains the only passage where he mentions these two other pillars of cenobitic life besides the monastery. Nevertheless, both of the Master's presentations of these topics have left more or less significant traces in Benedict's work. The Master's Prologue, which served to present the rule, furnished only the first word of Benedict's own Prologue: "*Obsculta…*" (Listen…), along with the idea of a journey toward God to which the reader is invited by the word he is going to hear. As for the huge first chapter of the Master's Rule, which ended with a ceremonious presentation of the abbot-teacher, Benedict preserves only its beginning where four kinds of monk are defined, beginning with cenobites. When he has reached the fourth kind — that of the gyrovagues — Benedict reproduces the definition while omitting the interminable satire the Master had developed on the theme, as well as the Master's discussion of the theory behind the abbot-teacher.

The beginning and end of the Prologue

Returning to the Prologue of the new Rule, we must take note of two remarkable facts concerning its beginning and end. These two "extremities", in fact, are equipped with brief original fragments. Here is the first:

> Listen, my son, to the precepts of a Master, and incline the ear of your heart. Accept with good spirit the exhortation of a loving father, and put it into practice, with the goal of returning, by the effort of your obedience, to Him from Whom you have been estranged by the laxity of disobedience. It is to you, whoever you are, that I address my speech, if, by renouncing your own wishes in order to serve the true King, Christ the Lord, you have taken up the powerful and glorious arms of obedience (Prologue, 1-3).

In this introduction, Benedict is not content merely to reproduce the appeal of the Master to "listen" or to evoke with his predecessor the journey towards God that is the result of such listening. He adds to the Master's suggestions the unmistakable echoes of the *Admonition to a Spiritual Son* attributed to St. Basil the Great. This pseudo-Basilian document not only began, like the prologues of our two Rules, with a plea to pay attention and understand, it also reproduced the Psalmist's invitation to "incline the ear" and—above all—spoke of "military service" for "Christ the King" and of taking up the spiritual "arms" of obedience to the leader's commands.

Benedict is thus plainly imitating this exordium of the *Admonition,* from which he takes the very word *admonitio* (translated as "exhortation" above) as well as the father-son relationship that he sets up between himself and his reader. And indeed the very first word of the Master, *"Listen..."*, launches a clear reminiscence of another, much more famous author. It matters little that this *Admonition to a Spiritual Son* is not, in fact, the work of Saint Basil himself, but of a Latin imitator, possibly born at Lerins around the year 500. If, as is probable, Benedict mistook the *Admonition* for a genuine work of Basil, the borrowing he made from it in the first lines of his Prologue amounts to a tacit homage to the famous monk-bishop from Cappadocia. Is it by chance that this Basilian beginning would be echoed in one of the last phrases of the epilogue, where Benedict recommends the *"Regula* of our Holy Father Basil"? In this way the entire Benedictine work is comprised between two references— one implicit, another explicit—to this illustrious predecessor, whose trademark can likewise be discerned throughout the intervening text in numerous passages of Cassinian legislation.

More significant still is the original paragraph that immediately precedes the last phrase of the Benedictine Prologue. After having reproduced the foundational decree of a "School of the Lord's Service" Benedict inserts the following personal comment:

> In organizing [the school], we hope to establish nothing
> harsh or burdensome. But if, as justice may require, some-
> thing rather restrictive is introduced for the purpose of cor-
> recting vices and preserving charity, do not hasten to flee
> from the path of salvation, which must begin by the nar-
> row gate. While advancing in the life of religion and faith,
> the heart expands, and we run along the path of God's com-
> mandments with the sweetness of an inexpressible love
> (Prologue, 46-49).

Resuming the discourse in the familiar second person with
which he had begun, Benedict renews in this way his characteristic qualities of affection and concern. Before concluding
his Prologue in the manner of the Master through the invocation of the sufferings of Christ in which the monk must patiently partake until death, the new legislator protests that he
does not want to impose anything too painful. According to
him, the way of salvation is *only narrow at the beginning*: a
rather bold paraphrase of Christ's statement, who simply said
that the way that leads to life is narrow, without any qualification (Matt. 7, 14).

But this apparent qualification of the Gospel text is justified
by what follows, when Benedict moves to the mystical level:
while it remains *objectively* restricted, the path of salvation
begins to widen by way of a *subjective* expansion. It is the
"heart" that becomes "larger" according to the word of the
Psalm (Psalm 118, 32), thanks to an "ineffable sweetness of
love", which in itself is evidence of the action of the Holy
Spirit (*cf.* Romans 8, 26).

Already this last addition to the Prologue makes us think
about the "spiritual lust" of the eternal life, to be treated in the
chapter on Good Works, as well as the "joy of the Holy Spirit"
and the "joy of spiritual desire" which spring forth, as we shall
see, from the observance of Lent. Going further, we can see
foreshadowed here the Rule's epilogue, where Benedict will

present the Rule as an elementary program for beginners who, to the degree that they advance toward perfection, intend to put into practice the most elevated teachings of the Holy Fathers. Like the conclusion of the Prologue, the conclusion of the entire Rule will be directed to the individual who intends to become a monk and it opens for him the same perspective on indefinite progress in union with God. When set beside the Rule of the Master, nothing is more characteristic of the Rule of Benedict than this dynamism, this spiritual drive toward the heights.

The abbot and the counsel of the brothers

The Master's treatment of the abbot's governance (*RM* 2), which followed his portrait of the abbot-teacher, formed a well-constructed discourse with matching beginning and end: as the Lord's representative in the monastery, the abbot must conform his teaching and governance to that of Christ, to whom he will render an account one day of the flock under his care. In between these two evocations of the Last Judgment, the abbot received a double lesson on two occasions: on the one hand, it was necessary for him to connect his personal example to his word, while taking care particularly to make himself as humble as a child; on the other hand, he had to treat the various sheep under his charge differently, each one according to his peculiar nature, while not failing to show the equal charity due to all.

At once both rigorous and flexible, this very harmonious plan of the Master has been treated a little roughly by Benedict (*Regula Benedicti* 2). Without going into every detail, we can clearly observe at least the disproportionate emphasis he gives to one of these themes: the diversity of treatment. Developed in two places by the Master, the same idea recurs no less than *four* times in Benedict, while the complementary theme of equal charity occurs only once. The image of the abbot also undergoes several retouchings: the new governance does not oblige him to be at the same time mother and father, nor to show himself as humble as a child. Instead, Benedict adds a useful warning against temporal anxieties which must not cloud the abbot's primary preoccupation with the salvation of souls. For the rest, the somewhat tedious insistence on the diversity of treatments has its point: it reveals a sense for the differences between persons in conjunction with a concern to help each one of them, which will reappear continually in the new Rule.

At the conclusion of his discussion of abbatial governance, the Master included instructions for an institution designed to assist the abbot in his direction: the consultation of the brothers. While following this suggestion of his predecessor, Benedict introduces two significant changes: he detaches it from the preceding chapter, and he completely rewrites it. The particular approach here — so unlike his usual method of recopying as seen in neighboring chapters — can be explained without hesitation by the special interest Benedict takes in legislative and practical affairs. While he is inclined to reproduce doctrinal statements with certain modifications only, when it comes to *praxis* he prefers to re-work things his own way. In this regard, the complete re-working of this passage on the consultation, placed in a separate chapter, foreshadows the next central part of the Rule (*RB* 8-66), where Benedict will cease his habitual copying of the Rule of the Master as he has done in the doctrinal chapters, and will recount all the rules of his predecessor in his own fashion.

The literary re-working, the first instance of which we can here detect, is accompanied by a number of spiritual and institutional changes. To begin with, Benedict doubles the Master's institution: he adds to the consultation of all the brothers of the community another smaller meeting, which includes only a few of the older brothers who assist the abbot in the less important questions. Furthermore, the purpose for consulting all the brothers has been remodeled. Instead of the two reasons considered by the Master who emphasized the need for good reasoning and fairness, Benedict has substituted what is really a supernatural motivation: "Often the Lord reveals to a younger person the best counsel ..."

Finally, the abbot and his brothers receive new admonitions. The abbot is at the outset put on guard against imprudence and injustice, and then is invited to observe the Rule and to think on the judgment of God, as if Benedict was afraid the abbot might in fact make a mistake — something not even envisaged by the Master! As for the brothers, they are prohibited from speaking with arrogance, from openly supporting their own suggestions, from following their own will and struggling with their abbot. These Benedictine innovations are doubtless to be explained by a longer experience of common life and its difficulties. The rather theoretical vision of the Master is confronted in Benedict's work by the givens of daily existence.

Maxims of the art of spirituality

Under a new title, "Instruments of Good Works" (*RB* 4), Benedict next reproduces the catalogue of maxims that constituted the Master's "holy art" (*ars sancta*). In the Master's Rule, these seventy-seven sentences were connected to the governance of the abbot to whom they offered guidelines, and were followed by a series of supplements: first, a bright description of Paradise, considered as the recompense promised to the artisans of the "holy art"; then two lists, of virtues to cultivate and vices to avoid; finally, some words on the monastery as a "workshop" where the spiritual art was to be practiced.

The Master's great collection of maxims is found again in Benedict's Rule slightly modified but without the description of Paradise or the lists of virtues and vices; Benedict only reproduces in conclusion the definition of the monastery as a "workshop". Thus reduced to almost half its original size, the "holy art" of the Master has undergone a good number of significant corrections. The trinitarian confession with which it opened is omitted (Did the version Benedict had before him even include it?) and the biblical commandment to honor father and mother has been changed into a maxim of hospitality ("honor all persons") as if the new legislator feared a recurrence of the familial relationships the monks had renounced.

One of the most interesting re-touches concerns the desire for eternity. "Desire eternal life *and Holy Jerusalem*", wrote the Master; "Desire eternal life *with all your spiritual concupiscence*", is how Benedict re-works it. This correction can best be explained by a concern for consistency: since he is going to omit the description of Paradise and the Heavenly Jerusalem with which the Master concluded his "holy art", Benedict avoids for the moment any mention of the future city. But the term he uses instead is full of meaning: if the monk ought to "desire eternal life with all his spiritual concupiscence", it is because such passion is the fruit of the Holy Spirit Who anticipates future blessings and fills the soul with joy. This "joy of spiritual desire" or "joy of the Holy Spirit" characterizes the struggle of Lent that yearns for Holy Easter which Benedict will describe in one of his most beautiful chapters.

The "spiritual concupiscence" here evoked recalls as well the "ineffable sweetness of love" at the end of the Prologue, where the epithet "ineffable" already suggested the action of the Holy Spirit. More generally, the present maxim reveals one of Benedict's distinctive traits: the interest he brings to *the way of doing things* and not merely to the things themselves. When he added "the Holy Jerusalem" to "the eternal life", the Master was adding a little bit of detail to the object desired. When Benedict replaces this objective detail with a subjective trait — "with all one's spiritual concupiscence" — he shows a concern that will reappear many times in his Rule: that of the interior quality of actions, something no less important than the actual accomplishment of the acts. The Master was preoccupied almost exclusively with tracing precise lines of behavior; Benedict is additionally committed to purifying and vivifying this behavior from within.

Other lesser changes made by the later author reveal other peculiar concerns. Evil thoughts ought not only "be broken against the Christ" but also should "be made known to an older spiritual man". It is necessary "to obey the commandments of the abbot" even if "he himself acts otherwise", because Benedict is much more aware than the Master of the human weakness of superiors. Further on, a series of maxims concerning interpersonal relations includes some supplements that proclaim one of the major innovations of the Benedictine Rule: the creation of an order of seniority whereby everyone has both "elders" he must "revere", and "younger ones" he must "love". Soon after, a new invitation to "pray for one's enemies" points ahead to the passage in the liturgical portion of the work where Benedict will prescribe to the superior the recitation in a loud voice of the *Our Father* twice a day, whereby each monk is summoned to forgive all those who have offended him.

In conclusion, Benedict replaces the Master's long and flowery description of the next world with a few words from the Apostle that evoke in a negative way "what no eye has seen or ear has heard, has God prepared for those who love Him" (1 Cor. 2,9). Operative here is not only Benedict's concern to *abbreviate* — something that marks the Benedictine Rule in its entirety — but also his preference for *scripture*, whereas the Master had taken his eschatological scenes from apocryphal passions and vision literature; there is also in Benedict a sense of the inexpressible character of the invisible realities of the next life as well as of spiritual experiences here below.

Obedience, silence, and humility

Continuing his work of abridgement, Benedict omits almost three-fourths of the chapter on obedience that he found in the Master (*RM* 7) and more than nine-tenths of the Master's closely connected pair of chapters on silence (*RM* 8-9).

The doctrine of obedience has been simplified (*RB* 5). The Master had set forth a dichotomy, with two forms of obedience — obedience without delay and obedience with delay — corresponding to perfect and imperfect subjects, respectively. For these, Benedict substitutes a unique ideal of immediate obedience which he proposes for all: "Who hears you, hears me" (Lk 10,16). These words of Christ which will be repeated in the conclusion of the chapter, make obedience to the superior an act of obedience to the Lord Himself.

Monastic obedience was presented by the Master as the "narrow way" of the Gospel, as the opposite of the "wide way" of seculars and bad monks who do only what they please. Here again, Benedict simplifies by eliminating all the satire on independent monks and even a large part of the praise of good monks. Nevertheless, he retains the Gospel citation that lies at the heart of the Master's commentary: "I have not come to do my own will, but the will of Him who sent me" (Jn 6,38). Christ is not only the one who commands the monk through the instrumentality of superiors (Lk 10,16); He is also the one who provides an example to the monk by doing the will of his Father.

To conclude, Benedict reproduces almost in its entirety the beautiful discussion of the Master on the interior qualities of obedience. He adds to it as well a threat of chastisement, which foreshadows the penal clauses that his Rule will have in abundance. His chapter on obedience is thus completed, happily abridging the Master while preserving the two Gospel citations that provide the foundation of the virtue of obedience, with Christ as the source of authority and Christ as the model of obedience.

The short chapter "On Silence" (*RB* 6) which follows the chapter on obedience is a drastic abridgement of two long chapters by the Master on this virtue. Neglecting from the outset the huge anthropological exposition of his predecessor, where various regions of the human composite are passed in review, Benedict only keeps what directly concerns the use of words. Silence appears here as a general means of avoiding the too frequent sins of the tongue, and as an attitude that suits the "disciple" who is the cenobitic monk, the monk who lives in community: it is the duty of the master, and thus the abbot, to speak and teach, while the disciple keeps quiet in order to listen.

The second aspect of silence, which weds it to obedience, becomes the object of a long legalistic dissertation by the Master, where detailed rules are set down for the verbal relationship between monk and abbot. Of this, Benedict keeps only the essential principle: it is necessary to address one's superior with humility and submission. At the same time, he reproduces with exact fidelity the Master's concluding phrases condemning all useless talk or jokes.

The Master's long chapter on humility (*RM* 10) is much less abbreviated than the rest and keeps more than half its content in Benedict's Rule (*RB* 7). Alongside its immediate source, the Benedictine treatise follows the discourse of the

Abbot Pinufius cited by Cassian in his *Institutes* (IV, 39). Just like the Master, Benedict transforms the ten signs of humility enumerated by Pinufius into the *twelve steps* of a ladder ascending from earth to heaven, the first and twelfth rungs pertaining to humility before God, the ten rungs in between pertaining to relations with fellow human beings.

The first degree of humility is particularly long and undergoes rather serious abridgement in the new Rule. The Master, in order to inculcate the fear of God and His all-seeing eye that misses nothing, passed in review five types of sins: sins of thought, of language, of the hands and feet, of willfulness, and of fleshly desires. At the beginning of his list, Benedict also enumerates five types, but afterwards, omitting faults of language, hands, and feet, passes directly from thoughts to the will and fleshly desires. This inconsistency is one of the clearest signs of the derivative nature of his version.

Further on, degrees five, eight, and ten, and above all degree three, have lost some of the scriptural citations with which they were illustrated. But these brief omissions are less important than the massive suppression of the Master's last page. In keeping with the image of the heavenly ladder taken from Jacob' dream in *Genesis* and providing the structure for the entire treatise on humility, the Master concluded with a splendid description of the "celestial homeland", taken from the *Passion of Saint Sebastian*. Benedict, however, suppresses the eschatological conclusion, just as at the end of the catalogue of good works. Here again, the Master's version is more coherent than his own: the heavenly "top" of the ladder, implied by the scriptural image, is missing in the later reworking.

Nevertheless, this inconsistency, caused by the need to abridge, has an important literary and doctrinal effect: it sets in relief the *terrestrial pole* of the ascent, namely the perfect charity that drives out fear. In the Master's Rule, this first term of the ascent was somewhat lacking, and the few lines that described it made a rather light impression before the long and brilliant description of paradise that we read soon after. Benedict, however, by dwelling on perfect charity, recovers the original conclusion of Pinufius, who did not speak at all about next-world compensation. Instead, the emphasis is on the value of spiritual progress here below, an emphasis we have already seen in his supplement to the prologue, and will see again in his epilogue.

One detail of this conclusion of the chapter on humility deserves to be mentioned: Benedict speaks here of the "love of Christ" which replaces the "fear of Gehenna" as a motive of good actions. This *amor Christi* is lacking in the Master, where the love of charity has for its object not the Christ, but the "good attitude" brought about by virtuous effort. From the love of the good one thus passes, in Benedict, to the love of the person of Christ. Coming after a mention of "God" (the Father) and before a mention of "the Holy Spirit", this homage to Christ lends a Trinitarian tone not only to the long chapter on humility but to the entire spiritual part of the Rule.

This concluding mention of the love of Christ recalls a peculiarity of the third degree of humility: it consists, according to the Benedictine version, in obedience "for the love of God". These words (*pro Dei amore*) are missing in the Master, and for good reason: it was only at the summit of the ladder, after the twelfth degree, that love had to enter the picture. By thus anticipating the point about love, Benedict once more commits a slight inconsistency, confirming that his version is not original. At the same time, however, he shows in a spontaneous way how divine charity is for him the supreme motive for obedience, and this is something he will state more than once in his Rule.

Chapter Three

The Treatise on the Divine Office

Immediately after the long chapter on humility—the crown of the spiritual portion of the Rule—Benedict takes up the regulation of the Divine Office (*RB* 8-20). The place he assigns to these chapters is all the more remarkable by the difference it shows from the arrangement of the Master, in which the treatise on the Office did not follow immediately after the doctrinal passages but began about twenty chapters later, after some long disquisitions on deans, excommunication, the cellarer, the tool-warden, the weekly service and the meal. Introduced through the discussion of the night-time vigil, the treatise on the Office (*RM* 33-49) occurred amidst the other actions of common life, between the monks' bedtime and their daily work. It did not appear as a task unique in its kind, or privileged.

By contrast, Benedict assigns a place of honor to "the work of God" (*opus Dei*) prior to any other occupation or concern. Such precedency accorded to the Office makes us think about the principle formulated later in the Rule concerning the exactitude of the hours of prayer: "Let nothing take precedence to the work of God". A quantitative measure provides further confirmation of the interest Benedict takes in the Office: his liturgical legislation represents well over half the number of pages the Master had devoted to the theme, even though Benedict's entire Rule is only about *one third* as long as the Master's.

The night before Sunday

Following the Master, Benedict begins with the regulation of the nightly offices, and finishes with two spiritual chapters on psalm-singing and prayer. But to be completely precise, it is necessary to point out that the Master's two last chapters in this section, entitled "Concerning behavior when one sings the psalms" and "On respect during prayer" (*RM* 47 and 48) were followed by a very brief note "On the monastic vigils", which prescribed passing the whole night before Sunday in psalm-singing and listening to readings (*RM* 49). Suppressing this little prescriptive conclusion, Benedict replaces it with a much fuller and more detailed chapter placed near the beginning of his treatise where he establishes a different observance: instead of the long Sunday vigil he substitutes a simple office for the end of nighttime, similar to the offices for ordinary days except longer: to the twelve psalms have been added twelve lessons and responses, three canticles from the Old Testament and a solemn reading from the Gospel, framed by two hymns of praise to the Trinity (*RB* 11).

This new arrangement clearly reflects the practice of the Church of Jerusalem, described a century and a half earlier by Egeria: for there, at the end of the night between Saturday and Sunday, three psalms were said and the Bishop read the gospel on the Resurrection. So Benedict, to set off this gospel-reading worthily, entrusts it to the abbot, has it preceded by the great Latin hymn *Te Deum laudamus,* and follows it by the short oriental hymn *Te decet laus.* Like the two seraphim from Isaiah, East and West are here united in their praise of the Triune God, Author of the Resurrection.

The Psalms of night and day

We just mentioned the twelve psalms, divided into two groups of six, which Benedict has the monks sing at all night offices. We can recognize here the quantity of psalms recommended by Cassian, according to whom the number twelve had been given to the first Egyptian monks by an angel who visited from heaven expressly to fix this number. Little heeded in his own country where the number of psalms was much increased, the abbot of Marseille was followed in Italy, both at Rome and at Monte Cassino. In this respect, Benedict does not differ significantly from the Master, whose quantity of psalms is the same, but he does affiliate himself more closely to the Egyptian tradition as conveyed by Cassian.

Twelve Psalms in the night office, three in the day office: on this last point as well, the new Rule shows its fidelity to the oriental usage advocated by the *Institutes* of Cassian, and it accords once again with the Rule of the Master and the Roman office. This sobriety contrasts with the prolixity of the daily psalmody in Provence, where Caesarius of Arles, Benedict's contemporary, was keeping the long celebrations of the Lerinian *ordo*, criticized by Cassian a century before.

The seven daily Offices and the hour of Prime

The law of the twelve nightly Psalms is not the only inviolable principle of the Benedictine Office. Two other regulations were fixed by Benedict as well: it is necessary to celebrate eight offices each day (*RB* 16) and recite the entire psalter every week (*RB* 18).

To be more precise, the new legislator, like the Master, wanted his monks to "praise" the Savior "seven times a day" (Ps. 118, 62). This interpretation of the word of the Psalmist, which takes "day" in the narrow sense of the twelve daytime hours, was not universal at that time. By taking "day" to mean the twenty-four hours of the legal day, some were restricting themselves to only seven daily offices including night vigils.

The epicenter of this debate was the Office of Prime. In order to safeguard Prime, Benedict insisted on the stricter interpretation of the "seven" as referring not just to a legal day but to the "daytime" day. The same concern to upgrade Prime explains the high relief Benedict gives to that office in the distribution of the weekly psalter which assigns to Prime particular psalms every day of the week, while the other short offices have the same allotment of psalms only five days out of seven.

The weekly Psalter

The weekly recitation of the psalter is, in fact, another one of Benedict's fundamental principles, requiring the precise distribution of all one hundred fifty psalms over the seven days of the week. In this point as in many others, he was inspired by the Roman Office from which nevertheless he removes much repetition and thereby shortens the length of the offices. To illustrate: in the smaller daytime offices, the Roman Office recited Psalm 118 in its entirety every day, with six sections assigned to each office, but Benedict spread this over two days (Sunday and Monday) thus reducing the number of sections recited at each hour from six to three. The remaining days of the week, from Tuesday through Saturday, at Terce, Sext, and None, the monks recited the nine short gradual psalms (Psalms 119-127) while Prime absorbed the beginning pieces of the psalter (Psalms 1,2, and 6), which the Roman Office had assigned to the vigil of Sunday.

On this point, Benedict differs from the Master who had the monks reciting the psalter in order, picking up at the beginning of each office where it had been left at the end of the preceding hour. This *psalterium currens* system is now replaced by the weekly psalter as practiced at Rome. However, the Roman Office, like that of the Master, required each psalm to be completely recited at each opportunity, while Benedict, following a suggestion by Cassian, divided the longer psalms into two, which once again had the effect of shortening the offices.

As in the Roman system, Benedict divides the psalter into two large parts. The first part, which extends to Psalm 108, supplies the pieces recited in the nightly offices, while the second part, beginning with Psalm 109, is for Vespers. From the first part, however, the new legislation sets aside (with a few exceptions) the first nineteen psalms for the hour of Prime; from the second part, the nine gradual psalms are set aside for the smaller offices. These preliminary subtractions are compensated in part by division of the longer psalms, yielding the twelve pieces needed for each nightly office. But the evening series is still insufficient and consequently Benedict reduces the number of psalms sung at Vespers from six to four.

Reference to the Roman Church

Such are the principal features of the Benedictine Office. Three major influences are visible: of the Master, of Cassian, and of Rome. Only the last of these is acknowledged. At Matins (the dawn office) after the first three psalms and before the last three psalms, Benedict has the monks recite a canticle from the Old Testament, a different one each day. Without discussing them in any detail, the legislator designates these verses as a kind of global reflection of Roman usage: *sicut psallit Ecclesia Romana* ("just as the Roman Church sings the psalms", *RB* 13, 10). A valued reference, which can be understood to apply to many other elements of the Benedictine Office as well.

The "Deus in adiutorium" at the beginning of the Hours

Since we have just had occasion to mention Cassian, we can recall yet another detail that leads us to think of the author of the *Conferences*. When Benedict prescribes at the beginning of each daily Office (*RB* 18, 1) the recitation of the psalm verse, "O God, come to my aid; Lord, hasten to help me", he is doubtless recalling the famous *Tenth Conference*, where Abbot Isaac recommended the ceaseless repetition of this verse in every circumstance of life. What Cassian intended as a formula to promote constant prayer, becomes a liturgical recitation for Benedict. From the individual effort to pray without ceasing, we pass to the community celebration of the hours. But there are other examples of a similar transfer. In the middle of the sixth century, Cassiodorus reports that the *Deus in adiutorium* was used as a ritual formula, and we shall see Benedict himself use it in this fashion. These distortions show both the success of Cassian's instruction and the partial failure of his attempt to revive continuous prayer.

The usage of the alleluia

As for the influence of the Master on Benedict, this too does not take place without many adaptations. This is why we find in the new code, as in the earlier one, the succession of the psalms "without alleluia" and psalms "with alleluia", but whereas the Master reserved the alleluia for the last third of the psalmody, Benedict extends it to cover the entire second half: six psalms without the alleluia are followed by six psalms with it. Moreover, this law is applied only to the night offices, while the Master's "law of the two thirds" was applied to all the offices.

The Problem of Praying the Psalms

One of the points where the comparison of the Benedictine Office with that of the Master still perplexes us today concerns the silent prayer that follows each psalm. Well attested as it is in the Master and in Cassian, was this traditional practice still in force at Benedict's monastery? When the latter conforms to the model offered by the Master in ending his liturgical section with two small chapters on spirituality, one on psalm-singing and one on prayer (*RB* 19-20; *cf. RM* 47-

48) we are encouraged to believe that Benedict had in view the same two elements in the source Rule that followed one after the other without ceasing in the course of the monastic office of earlier centuries. But the second of the two chapters entitled, "On reverence during prayer", appears to envisage the prolongation of individual prayer under the effect of divine inspiration, something clearly located outside the framework of the community office. And when Benedict in the following phrase returns to the community framework ("However, in the assembled community… [*in conventu tamen …*]) is he here implying psalm-prayer, which he does not ever mention clearly elsewhere in the Rule, or is he thinking of some other kind of prayerful silence, held in common, for example, at the end of each hour of the Office?

This question is all the more pressing since the ancient custom of stopping and praying after the psalm is still attested in seventh century Gaul. At the end of all the psalms, Columbanus asks for every monk to recite privately a triple *Deus in adiutorium* — and this, by the way, is another example of a liturgical use of this formula — and then Donatus reduces these three invocations to one only. If Gallic monasticism keeps these traces of psalm-prayer after Benedict's day, would Benedict himself have abolished this traditional observance which he found described by the Master?

The authorization to redistribute the Psalter

Just before concluding his treatment of the Office with his chapters on psalmody and prayer as we have just discussed, Benedict makes a declaration which deserves notice. After having minutely determined, in his rather long Chapter 18, which Psalms ought to be said each hour of every day, he goes on to arrange the weekly distribution of psalms as follows:

> Above all, we must state this admonition: if someone does not like this distribution of the psalms, let him arrange them

some other way that seems fitting to him. But let him make very sure to recite the entire psalter every week, with all one hundred fifty Psalms, and let him be sure to start all over again each Sunday in the vigil office. For the monks show too little zeal for the service they have entered if they recite less than the entire psalter every week, along with the usual canticles. Since we read that our holy Fathers had heroically accomplished this in a single day, as luke-warm as we are, we should still be able to do it in a week (RB 18, 21-25).

A very clear distinction is being drawn here between what is essential and what is merely accessory. The only thing Benedict is absolutely requiring is the recitation of the entire psalter within a single week. As for the distribution of the psalms over the various offices, he proposes his own method as only one possible means of doing it.

The feat accomplished by "Our Holy Fathers" which Benedict alludes to in conclusion is handed down in a Greek apothegm that had been translated into Latin. According to this story, a hermit paid a visit to another monk. Before taking their evening meal, the two men decided to pray to God. One of them recited the entire psalter, the other recited two major prophets. When they were finished, it was daybreak and the visitor returned from whence he had come: they had both forgotten to eat!

Both humorous and edifying, this little tale reports a unique event, something that happened once, and not a custom. The recitation of the entire Psalter in a single day does not appear in any way to have been a "custom" of the ancients, to which one could oppose the weekly recitation of the Psalms as pre-scribed by the Rule. Consequently, the argument Benedict derives from this anecdote is not in the least convincing. But his recourse to the "heroism" of "our Holy Fathers", intended as a reproach to the "lukewarmness" of the monks of his day, is no less meaningful for all that. It shows how Benedict was vividly aware of the distance between the observances of his own generation and the observances of the original monks. This discrepancy is felt as a decadence, and the legislator invokes it not so much to provoke improvement as to ward off any further decline.

We will find the same pessimistic view of history founded on the same anecdote collection, in a later passage where Benedict discusses the use of wine. There again, the unapproachable rigor of the Fathers will be invoked in order to enforce a minimum of decency on the monks of Benedict's own day. And in his last chapter, the author of the Rule will complain once more about the decadence of his own time, which causes him to "blush with shame" and which he hopes to stem by publishing his "very small Rule for beginners".

These two anecdotes that Benedict cites in regard to the topics of psalm recitation and the use of wine, lead us to suspect that his admiration for the monks of the past derives from his reading. At the very time when he was composing his Rule, the Roman Deacon Pelagius, the future Pope, had just completed a partial translation of a systematic collection of apothegms he had come across in Palestine and brought back with him to Italy. It is from this work that Benedict appears to have nourished, if not actually *acquired*, that sense of inferiority to the past that he is so eager to convey to his readers for the purpose of reforming them.

Chapter Four

Deans–Dormitory–Penal Code

After treating the Divine Office, Benedict takes up three apparently independent questions that were closely connected with each other by the Master. For the latter had appended to his long chapter on provosts (deans or "superiors of ten men each") a section on the dormitory, the place where these superiors exercise their surveillance; the Master had done something similar before, when he added to his discussion of the abbot an appendix on the consultation of the brothers, convoked and supervised by the abbot (*RM* 11). Immediately after these points, then, the Master entered the domain of the penal sanctions that result from insubordination of the brothers toward their superiors.

Subordinate officers (*decani,* known as "provosts" or "deans") the common dormitory, excommunication: these three connected subjects, which the Master ruled on (in that order) at the beginning of his section on practical matters, are found in Benedict's Rule immediately after his treatment of the Office. Dispensing with certain explicit connections established by his predecessor, the new legislator presents the first two questions in distinct chapters (*RB* 21-22). He then embarks on the discussion of the penal code, whose divisions are multiplied, despite being severely abridged: the four chapters of the Master on penance have become eight in Benedict.

The Deans or "Seniors"

Two strictly equal officers, whom the Master called "provosts" (*praepositi*), were placed at the head of each group of ten brothers. More vaguely, the new Rule speaks of "deans" (*decani*), a term that also implies a group of ten men (*cf.* Latin *decem*) but something remains unclear: is the leader of each group—only one person, apparently—himself *included* in the number ten (this was the case with the Egyptian cenobites Jerome described in 384) or is he *added* to them, as with the Master? The name "dean" (*decanus*) is only used in this passage and at the very end of the Rule; the two chapters that follow will refer to them as "elders" (*seniores*).

The Master had placed utmost importance on the educating role of the provosts, as veritable teaching assistants or proctors in charge of watching over their men at every moment, unceasingly conveying the abbot's instructions and immediately correcting every transgression of these precepts that emanated from a master accredited by God himself. Nine types of warning, correlated to an equal number of small particular delinquencies, illustrated this function of the correctors.

But Benedict, without detailing the pedagogical action of the deans, restricts himself to delegating to them the all-around "care" of their deaneries. And yet, while drastically abridging the text of his predecessor, the new legislator insists on the qualities required by those chosen to be deans, and he foresees an eventuality the Master never dreamed of: if a dean becomes proud and refuses to correct himself, he must be taken from office and be replaced. A shift of interest has occurred from the earlier Rule to the later: in place of a detailed catalogue of the failings of subordinates who have been entrusted to the surveillance of irreproachable leaders, we see anxiety about possible failings in the leaders themselves! This new concern recalls the advice given to the abbot about the counsel of the brothers (*RB* 3).

The educational theory according to which the Master had designed his monastery/school assumed practically impeccable masters. But this theoretical perfection of the abbot and his cooperators is questioned by the new legislator whose realistic vision, formed by his experience, takes account of serious divergences between the ideal and the real.

The common dormitory

The transition from individual sleeping cells to a common dormitory, which took place toward the end of the fifth century, was the major event in the history of community religious life in antiquity. The main reason for it was the need to keep a better watch on the monks, tempted as they were to use their private cells for hiding faulty behavior. The Master is one of the earliest witnesses of the new discipline, which reunited the entire community in a single place, where nothing could escape the eyes of the superiors.

This nightly surveillance by the deans was the reason why the Master had dealt with the dormitory in the conclusion of his chapter on the provosts (*praepositi*). Benedict also makes mention of it but only in a cursory manner. Apart from the Rule of the Master, we can also think of the famous description of Egyptian community life as sketched out by Jerome in 384, in his letter to Eustochium (*Epistle* 22, 35), wherein the future superior at Bethlehem depicts with such amusement the nightly visits of the deans to the sleeping-cells of their men, to encourage them to stay awake.

From the time of the Master to that of Benedict, the communities seem to have grown in size since we now visualize several dormitories, each one holding about ten or twenty brothers. Like his predecessor, Benedict requires that they sleep with their clothes on, and that their apparel not include the knife in their belt. Similar to the reasoning of the Master as well is Benedict's reasoning for making them sleep fully clothed: to get ready quickly for the night office, and at this point the monks are invited to help the cause by discreetly encouraging each other to get up. Another reason that seemed important to the Master—that a sleeping monk not touch his own naked body—is omitted by Benedict.

But not only are the brothers supposed to encourage each other mutually in moving as quickly as possible from their beds to the oratory: in addition he asks each one to "hurry past" the other. The reservation that accompanies this instruction—that they do this "with all gravity and restraint"—probably explains the recommendation that follows: "Let the younger brothers not have their beds next to one another". The legislator is taking precaution against juvenile "races" and other kinds of unseriousness.

But this detail is less important than one global truth: to the end of promoting good conduct among the brothers, Benedict not only has recourse to observation by superiors; he also looks to the influence they can have *on each other*. This is Benedict sketching into the picture his own new theme of fraternal relationships, so unlike the Master—a theme given ever more precise affirmation as he proceeds.

Two other innovations by Benedict appear in this passage. One of them—the constantly burning light in the dormitory—is found in a later chapter of the Master but the second is without parallel in its source-text: Benedict requires that the abbot give to each monk "bedding suited to his personal discipline". Such at least appears to be the meaning of the rather opaque expression *pro modo conversationis*; we see here the very important word *conversatio* which is used time and again for the monks' way of life, collective or personal, as seen in relation to their ideal and their commitments.

Correction of faults and love of the faulty ones

The eight chapters that follow (*RB* 23-30) treat of excommunication and its consequences. Just like the Church, the monastery "excommunicates" those who commit serious misdeeds, with the purpose of encouraging their repentance and of preventing any contamination of their brethren.

The greater part of the prescriptions Benedict makes in this area could already be read in the Master, but the latter also clothed his penal law in full ceremonial procedure, where rhetoric held a considerable place. Once someone was reported to the abbot by the *praepositi*, he would receive a long reprimand from him, and was required to make a long speech of supplication for himself after each psalm in the office, addressed to the community and to his superior in order to obtain their pardon for his offense. The ceremony of reconciliation was followed by a no less lengthy prayer by the excommunicated monk and a final admonition by the abbot.

Omitting all these discourses, Benedict is content to regulate excommunication here, and postpone to a later chapter (*RB* 44) the satisfaction and the reconciliation of the excommunicated monk. Like the Master, he distinguishes lesser faults for which one is excluded from the community *meal* only, and more serious ones, which entail exclusion from the community's *prayer* as well.

In this Benedictine abridgement certain new details appear, but we must especially take note of two brand new chapters (27-28) where the author provides the abbot with a pastoral method for leading the wayward party back to his senses. Likened to a physician, the abbot should use various remedies, beginning with sending older, wiser brothers, called *senpectae* [Greek, of disputed meaning] to speak with him, who present themselves as comforters and encourage the wayward by their sympathetic counsel to make humble satisfaction. Benedict twice instructs the abbot and the brothers to pray as a community for the healing of the sick. If it should end in someone's exclusion in case he refuses to repent, this is done "in order to keep one bad sheep from infecting the entire flock".

Physical blows are not ruled out of this therapy. They are administered when the excommunicated monk is obstinate in his error, and also when someone by reason of youth or lack of intelligence is simply not capable of understanding what the spiritual punishment of excommunication means. These considerations on excommunication and corporal punishment could be read already in the Master. Similarly, even he included a sorrowful speech to be made by the penitent to the abbot which evokes the figure of the Good Shepherd who leaves the entire flock in search of the lost sheep. However, when Benedict in his turn proposes this Gospel example of loving concern for the wayward, his exhortation has something more serious and moving about it.

The next to the last chapter of this penal section (29) considers the case of the return of a brother who has left the monastery through his own fault. He can be admitted no more than three times. Here too, Benedict follows the Master who states the same norm of three readmissions at another place in his Rule (*RM* 64). But the new legislation imposes two new conditions: the brother who wants to re-enter must promise to amend himself and accept being relegated to the lowest rank. This second condition is meant to test his humility, in accordance with a characteristic emphasis of the Benedictine Rule: never to let pass an opportunity to promote humility.

Chapter Five

The Cellarer; Food and Drink

When Benedict follows his discussion of the penal code with the themes of the cellarer and others responsible for material things, and then of the weekly menu, he follows the Master's treatment step by step. But he adds something rather new by consecrating two chapters in succession to the complete renouncing of all possessions by the brothers and the distribution of necessities according to needs. The Master treated only the first of these two subjects and included it as a paragraph within his instructions for the cellarer.

Another innovation appears a little later, when Benedict constructs a specially distinct chapter entitled, "Of Sick Brothers", which comprises the measures which the Master directed to be taken on their behalf within his chapter on fasts. In this case, too, then, our Lawgiver found elements in the older Rule that reappear in his new chapters on renunciation and the sick.

The cellarer and the keepers of utensils

Much less precise and circumstantial than the Master on these matters (*RM* 16), Benedict provides little direction on the concrete tasks of the cellarer, but shows a new and different interest in the relationship between this officer and the other brothers (*RB* 31). Again and again he instructs the cellarer to avoid angering by abrupt denials those who ask for more, to avoid conflicts by at least giving a "good answer" in the unavailability of what they are asking for, and never to show arrogance or to keep them waiting. In two places the cellarer is invited to cultivate humility, the virtue that makes for easier communication.

On the other side, the new lawgiver is anxious that the cellarer be provided with working conditions that do not overtax him. Assistants should be given to him if the community is a large one, and a schedule should be established in order to preserve peace. The admirable final sentence—"…that no one be troubled or saddened in the House of God"—sums up the moral content of Benedict's chapter, where the practical tendencies of the Master give way to spiritual direction that recalls the words of an abbot. Indeed, just like the abbot, the cellarer is supposed "to take care of the sick, the children, guests, and the poor with all his solicitude, knowing that he will have to render account for each of these persons on the day of judgment." A material task has never been more closely assimilated to the pastoral function of someone responsible for souls!

As with the Master (*RM* 17) the keepers of utensils and monastery belongings form the subject of a much shorter chapter, where Benedict is content to give a minimum of very modest instructions (*RB* 32). There are two principal novelties: instead of the Master's lone keeper there are several (the sign of a larger community?) and finally, a penal sanction attaches to any negligence, as so often seen at the end of chapters of the Benedictine code.

The common ownership of goods

Treating here the individual renunciation of possessions and the unequal distribution of what is needed (*RB* 33-34), Benedict follows a suggestion of the Master who at the end of his chapter on the cellarer recalled the law of the renunciation of all personal property. But the new legislation is different from this through its reference to the *Acts of the Apostles*: if nobody in the monastery possesses anything of his own, it is because of their desire to imitate the first community of the faithful in Jerusalem who "held everything in common", without anyone daring to consider anything as his own (*Acts* 4,32).

It is true that the Master elsewhere invokes the primitive Church, but this is only in an allusion to Ananias and Saphira (*RM* 82. 20-21). He never formally proposes the community at Jerusalem as a model. In citing the famous verses from *Acts*, the Benedictine Rule affiliates itself rather to the Rule of St. Augustine who evokes the perfect *communio* of the primitive Church at the outset, including its distribution of the necessities "to each according to his needs" (*Acts* 4,34). In the style of Augustine, Benedict presents the particular needs as infirmities for which there is every reason to humble oneself, while those who are less fortunate ought to rejoice in their ability to be content with the minimum.

Such Augustinian considerations, lacking in the Master, tend to develop a sense for the diversity of persons and a concern for good relations among the brothers which Benedict sums up in the word "peace". The guidelines for the cellarer already insisted on fraternal relationships. This preoccupation with good mutual understanding, a novelty with respect to the Master's Rule, will characterize Benedict's entire work.

The weekly food service and the infirmary

Kept in reserve by the cellarer, the community's sustenance is prepared and served day in, day out, by kitchen servants who are relieved every week by another crew (*RB* 35). A lector also on duty for a week at a time takes care that spiritual nourishment is likewise to be found in the refectory (38). While taking these functions from the Master who was himself inspired by Cassian, Benedict adds to them a permanent infirmarian (36) of which neither the Master nor Cassian had made mention.

This section, like the previous one, is stamped with a concern for mutual charity that was missing in the Master. Almost all the many practical details of the latter are left out, but Benedict remarks insistently that the food service is a work of charity. We find here too Benedict's anxiety to help the weak, whether by making sure they have help or by granting all the servers a supplement of food and drink an hour before the community meal.

The chapter on the sick, which is almost entirely new, manifests to the utmost degree Benedict's concern for establishing and maintaining affectionate relationships among the brothers. The *moral* infirmities of the sick are to be borne with patience, and reciprocally, the sick have to strive especially hard not to be a burden on the brothers who serve them for the love of Christ. And even though the lawgiver urges the abbot to be particularly vigilant toward the sick, he also provides for them himself, giving them their own place and an infirmarian with his own title (*servitor...diligens ac sollicitus*); both these features are lacking in the Master. Equally novel are the refinements Benedict makes concerning baths and meat.

Regulation of food and dispensations

In the final chapters of this section on food, drink and the dinner-hour (*RB* 39-41; *cf. RM* 26-28), one of the remarkable facts is the shift of motivation for granting liquid or solid supplements to the community. For the Master, such exceptional favors enhanced the meaning of feast days; with Benedict, they come as remedies for the fatigue of work. This change which goes hand in hand with the new authorization given by Benedict to field-labor is doubtless connected to the harsher economic climate of the times, when Italy was under the affliction of the Gothic-Byzantine wars.

In matters concerning food, Benedict shows a certain reserve that was absent from the other Rule: the two cooked dishes which he recommends just as the Master did are not offered both together, but by choice. This restrictive tendency shows itself more clearly in the following chapter "On the regulation of drink" where Benedict encourages the brothers to abstain from wine, citing a saying of old that "wine is not for monks". This apothegm was taken, as was that other one about reciting the entire Psalter in one day, from a systematic collection newly translated from the Greek by the deacon Pelagius. Benedict seems to have been impressed by these wonderful sayings of the ancients, which make him look on the less severe habits of the monks of his own day as a decline from something greater.

Chapter Six

From the Divine Office
to Manual Labor

Immediately after his regulation of the time for dinner, the Master went on to speak about the siesta following dinner, about the silence of the dormitory after Compline and then about the announcement of day and night duties. These three small chapters are preparatory for the treatment of the Divine Office at the beginning of which the Master determined the modes of rising in the morning and the schedule of the night office.

Many elements of this sequence reappear in Benedict, who likewise follows his chapter on fasts with prescriptions about observing silence after Compline, and likewise, a little later, rules on the announcement of duties. But the treatise on the Divine Office, we may recall, had been placed by Benedict directly after the chapter on humility, in a place of honor that makes the Divine Office of primary concern in the practical part of the Rule. As if to fill up the vacancy where it had been, Benedict here inserts — between the chapter on silence after Compline (42) and the announcement of the chores (47) — a treatise on satisfaction, showing how various failings can be made up for: lateness, first, then the (more or less) serious faults meriting excommunication, then shortcomings in the celebration of the Office, and finally every kind of external accident. And in contrast with these, the new Rule also mentions, in closing, faults of the soul which must be repaired — not by public satisfaction but by private confession, made to a spiritual father.

At first sight, this ensemble of four chapters on the repair of shortcomings (*RB* 43-46) appears somewhat random, not seeming to have any connection with what precedes and follows. But its presence right here is explained by a detail of the Rule of the Master. For, at the beginning of his treatise on the Office, the Master had penalized lateness to nighttime prayer (*RM* 32, 9-15). So now Benedict, even though he has already dealt with the Divine Office, still keeps in its former place the measures to be taken against lateness to the oratory as the first type of failings penalized in these four chapters.

Reading before Compline

Beginning with a lovely general maxim "At all times, monks ought to cultivate silence", the chapter where Benedict prohibits speaking after Compline (*RB* 42) is distinguished from the same place in the Master by a new directive: before celebrating the last office of the day, the brothers ought to listen to an edifying reading—"of four or five pages", the lawgiver specifies—taken from the *Conferences* or the *Lives of the Fathers*.

Already prescribed by the Augustinian *Ordo Monasterii* from which Benedict must have taken it directly, this practice not only represents a trace of influence of Augustine's Rule on the Rule of Benedict; also, by encountering Cassian's *Conferences* as the first example of an "edifying" reading, we are allowed to see Benedict's personal loyalty to the great author of Provence, whence came (by way of the Master) the clearest part of his spiritual doctrine. And when he adds *The Lives of the Fathers* to Cassian's *Conferences* he is certainly thinking above all of a work which bears this title and which he has cited twice with veneration: the systematic collection of apothegms recently translated by the deacon Pelagius.

The *Conferences* of Cassian report conversations of the author with Egyptian solitaries and the apothegms translated by Pelagius emanate from the same Egyptian anchorite milieu.

From the Divine Office to Manual Labor

The mention of these two types of reading therefore indicate the direction we need to look if we want to find Benedict's principal inspiration. He will return to the subject in his epilogue where the *Institutes* of Cassian are added to the *Conferences* and the *Lives of the Fathers,* and the whole Egyptian group is rounded out by the Cappadocian Rule of Saint Basil.

"Put nothing before the Work of God"

In the following chapter, where the late are penalized (*RB* 43) Benedict is led to this topic not only (as we have pointed out) by the corresponding passage of the Master (*RM* 32) on those who are late to the nighttime Office. Two other chapters of the source Rule have also made a contribution: one (*RM* 54) described the promptness with which the brothers were supposed to respond to the Office signal, the other (*RM* 73) penalized those arriving late to the "Work of God" (or Divine Office) day or night, and also those who were late to dinner.

However, when he begins his instructions with the immediate response to be given to the signal that announces the nighttime Office, Benedict is also recalling clearly a more ancient text: The Second Rule of the Fathers which is known with certainty to have been elaborated at Lerins in 427. In this text is found the axiom, "Let nothing be put before prayer," where the celebrated maxim of Cyprian, "Put absolutely nothing before Christ", receives a particular application and readiness to do the Work of God is taken as a sign of the love of Christ.

This Second Rule from Lerins also makes us think of one of Benedict's recommendations in the course of his chapter on late-comers. When he requires that the late-comer (he is speaking of night office) enter the oratory rather than stand at the door, lest he become subject to gossip, we can recognize here the fear of gossip (*fabulae*) expressed on one occasion in the Second Rule, a propos of those who leave the oratory during the nighttime office.

The Work Schedule and Reading

When Benedict proceeds from this to the regulation of the daily horarium (*RB* 48) he begins as the Master did by inculcating the necessity for work, but his much shorter reworking only mentions the first motivation for work given by his predecessor: the avoidance of laziness, and passes by in silence the other purpose of manual labor: to have something to give to the poor (*RM* 50, 1-7). Only the ascetic purpose of work is named, while its charitable purpose disappears.

Another important modification by Benedict is the permission to perform agricultural labor. This had been rejected by the Master toward the end of his Rule (*RM* 86) for fear of harming the contemplation of the monks and lest it compromise monastic fasting. In authorizing his sons to bring in the harvest themselves, the new lawgiver is doubtless giving way to the economic pressures of the very difficult contemporary situation. All the same, he calls on the authority of "our Fathers" and "the Apostles" in affirming that such labor is characteristic of "true monks". This recourse to the example of "the Fathers" — and this means the first generations of monks — shows once again the traditionalism of Benedict and his attachment to the primitive monasticism of Egypt and elsewhere, reflected in particular by the writings of Cassian and the apothegms.

When it comes to reading — the other major occupation of the monks — the new lawgiver shows himself less generous than his predecessor: in winter as well as in summer the hours of reading are reduced to two, Lent being the only time when the full three hours are allowed, which the Master had permitted in all seasons. Furthermore, Benedict judges it necessary to institute patrols to make sure the brothers are not wasting this time chatting or lounging about.

As with the Master, the reading is to be done at the beginning of the day in winter, but in summer, instead of

From the Divine Office to Manual Labor
being put off to the end of the day, the reading is scheduled at
the last hours of morning, before the meal which in that season
is normally at midday. This order, through which spiritual
nourishment is taken just before corporeal nourishment, recalls
the Augustinian *Ordo Monasterii*, in which the dinner hour
was fixed at the ninth hour (*nona*) throughout the year so that
the reading which immediately preceded it, took place early
in the afternoon.

Even though he reduces the weekly time for reading,
Benedict makes it into an obligation every Sunday, while
the Master had left Sunday completely free. Another innovation by Benedict is to give up on the Master's organized group-
reading, whereby one brother in each group of ten would
read aloud while the others listened. By all appearances, the
Benedictine Rule lets each monk read on his own. This individual reading is even explicitly prescribed for Lent, when
each brother is to receive a codex from the library which he is
supposed to read in order from beginning to end.

One of the salient features of the Benedictine horarium is
its complexity. Instead of basing his use of time simply on the
great articulations of the civil and ecclesiastical day (Terce,
Sext, None) as did the early monks as well as the Master,
Benedict on several occasions advances or delays these hours
of the Office in order to give reading and manual labor the
varying length of time he thinks necessary. This concern for
the "right amount of time for everything" is not without a certain
re-arranging of the Divine Office: its schedule, instead of placing
a limit on activities, becomes pliant to what these activities
demand.

Chapter Seven

Lent; External Relations

We will connect our discussion of the chapter on Lent to the chapters that follow it; but if we keep in view the Rule of the Master, we see that in many ways the theme is connected to the preceding pages where both the Master and Benedict have been setting out the daily horarium. The "Lenten Observance" (as the Master calls it) begins in his work with a series of guidelines having to do with the use of time; during Lent, in the middle of each interval between two offices, all the brothers meet to make a common silent prayer. It is only after establishing this cycle of "prayers without psalms" that the Master treats of the discipline for food and other particulars of Lent.

Following the arrangements for Lent, the Rule of the Master passed in review a number of different questions, beginning by commenting on the manner of behaving when hindered from getting to the oratory for the Office or when absent from the monastery. Without meaning to reduce to a unity this miscellany of diverse topics, one could in summary say that the Master's dominant theme in these chapters was that of the monks' exiting the monastery and engagement with the outside world.

The observance of Lent

Prayer and abstinence: these two principal elements of the Lenten program traced out by the Master (*RM* 51-53) are to be found in a corresponding chapter in Benedict (*RB* 49) but under a very different form. In place of common prayers fixed by the Rule and carried out at regular intervals, the new legislation invites each brother to "pray with tears", as he thinks fit, and to make "private prayers" when it seems a good idea. The "abstinences" of food and drink are likewise left to the discretion of each, taking account of the regular observance that was previously established. For the Master, these things were more closely supervised.

Beyond such food and drink restrictions (to which we can add deprivations of sleep) Benedict invites the monks to reduce their speech and amusements as well. Above all, he adds to the regular corporal mortifications a properly spiritual effort of reading and contrition of heart. Penances themselves ought to be offered to God with the joy of the Holy Spirit (1 Thess 1.6) and the entire Lenten discipline is carried out "awaiting holy Eastertide, with the joy of a spiritual desire". These instructions, which call to mind a Benedictine spirituality in the most precise sense (*RB* 4, 46: "To desire eternal life with all one's spiritual passion") tends to the rehabilitation of desire itself, whereas the doctrinal part of the Rule of the Master spoke only of "carnal desires" or "evil desires".

The same inflection can be seen in regard to the "individual will", so often condemned before, and now presented as the source of meritorious Lenten sacrifices. Even so, Benedict is careful when concluding to make all these spontaneous offerings subject to the approval of the abbot, lest the monks become vainglorious and presumptuous.

Prayer and meals outside the monastic framework

Along the same line of submission to the abbot, Benedict reserves to the latter's authority the permission for a brother to be exempted from the common office for reason of work (*RB* 50). The Rule of the Master specified fifty paces as the distance that would dispense a worker from coming to the office. Omitting this precision, the Benedictine Rule leaves the matter entirely to the Abbot's decision.

Similarly, it is solely permission of the abbot that can authorize any eating outside the monastery, when a monk has been sent on a mission (*RB* 51). Benedict thereby resolves in a few words a problem that is debated at length by the Master, whose complex casuistry paves the way for a rather simple law.

The oratory of the monastery

Although there is apparently no connection between these two small chapters and what Benedict has to say next about the monastery's oratory (*RB* 52) the location here of these remarks on the place of prayer is explained by an association of ideas which connect the corresponding chapter of the Master (*RM* 68) to the observations he had made on departures in the chapter preceding. In fact, it is at the departure from the oratory, when the office was over, that the Master required everyone to be silent in the holy place. This requirement had been suggested to him by the ceremony he had just discussed: the brother who returns from a journey ought to recommend himself to the prayers of the brothers during the office and receive from them the kiss of peace at its conclusion (*RM* 67).

The comparison of the Benedictine text with its source reveals surprisingly that in this one place Benedict writes at longer length than the Master. This is because he is here adding the authority of Augustine to his usual source: Benedict owes to Augustine his concern to protect individual prayer made outside the schedule of the Office by excluding any noise in the oratory that could impede it.

"Not with a shrill voice, but with tears and diligence of the heart": these modalities of prayer proclaimed by Benedict make us think of Cassian. In this way, a ceremonial regulation by the Master—that the departure from the oratory after a common Office must be carried out in silence—is changed into an exhortation to prayer, where the reminiscences of Augustine and Cassian are mingled with Benedict's own views on prayer as he formulated them at the end of his treatise on the Office and on the chapter on Lent (*RB* 20 and 49).

The reception of guests

In a full treatment of hospitality (*RB* 53) Benedict next assembles remarks of the Master that are dispersed through four different chapters (*RM* 65; 71-72; 79) while completely omitting a fifth chapter (*RM* 78) which prescribed manual labor for every guest staying longer than two days.

A certain difference of tone can be felt between the beginning of the treatise where we hear of nothing but veneration for the guest who must be received with faith and eagerness like Christ in person, and the rest of the treatise where several caveats appear: first, the guests must not disturb the community life; to avoid this, only the abbot sits down to eat with them, at a special time, with food prepared in a separate kitchen; secondly, apart from those responsible for hospitality, no one is authorized to speak with the guests. This limitation of relationships between the brothers and the guests recalls the Rule of the Four Fathers, while the initial enthusiasm with which they are received is clearly inspired by the *Historia Monachorum*.

Among the innovations of Benedict, we may take note of the creation of a permanent host or hotelier, who replaces the two temporary officers the Master had established.

*Clothing, renunciation of property, distribution of
necessities*

In the following chapter (*RB* 54) which owes nothing at all
to the Master, Benedict combines two passages from the Rule
of St. Augustine, where Augustine forbade secretly receiving
letters or presents from a woman and any items offered by
the monk's family. In the latter case, the superior could divert
the thing to someone other than the intended receiver.
Benedict's rehearsal of these two Augustinian prohibitions
prepares the way for the long chapter that follows on the
monks' clothing and shoes, which concludes with Benedict's
opposition to any ownership even of necessary things.

This chapter on the dress-code and renunciation of property (*RB* 55) correspond exactly to the two succeeding chapters of the Master who regulates the same two matters (*RM*
81-82). But while not leaving out anything said by his predecessor, Benedict adds several new principles to his own legislation. One of them is taken from the Rule of Basil: materials
and colors depend on the region one happens to live in; they
must be content with what is locally the less expensive. In the
same spirit of adaptation to different places and climates, the
legislator yields his authority to the local superior who alone is
qualified to decide what is necessary in each case. The abbot
is also to see that the clothing is the right size for the wearer.

One of Benedict's special concerns is the avoidance of any
kind of possessions: each time someone receives something
new, he has to turn in the old thing. The abbot is commis-
sioned to "inspect the beds frequently" where they could be
hiding unauthorized items, just as the Master wanted his pre-
fects to "inspect" their men "frequently" to take away whatever they would have acquired. But just as before (*RB* 33-
34) Benedict joins to the prohibition of any property a sum-
mons to the corresponding duty of the abbot: "to give to ev-

eryone according to his need" (*Acts* 4, 35). An interesting list of ten things illustrates this principle: in addition to the garments and shoes, each monk is to have "knife, pen, needle, towel and writing tablets"—affording us a glimpse of how the scribal labor in particular was considered "necessary".

The abbot's table and the artisans of the monastery

To conclude this section, Benedict follows the Master in handling two questions whose common purpose is the placing of the monks into relation with people outside the monastery. In regard to the abbot's table (*RB* 56) the new legislation merely repeats the earlier (*RM* 84): the regular dining companions of the superior, who are guests, can be replaced by any brothers the abbot may choose to invite, except that the deans must still remain at their tables.

The chapter on artisans is more original (*RB* 57). We find there, in reverse order, two preoccupations of the Master (*RM* 85): the selling of monastic products at a low price and the avoidance of all dishonesty in such selling. But Benedict adds to each of these principles a new scriptural illustration— the example of Ananias and Saphira for dishonesty and for the pricing—the lovely concluding maxim, "Let God be glorified in all things" (1 Peter 4,11). Furthermore, he begins his chapter by posing a characteristic condition: the artisan ought to remain humble, and for this reason the abbot, who has given him the authorization to exercise his skill, can and must remove him from that occupation should he ever prove arrogant.

Chapter Eight

The Renewal of the Community; the Abbacy

Omitting the Master's chapter on the monastery's tenant-farms (*RM* 86) which no longer have to be recommended since the new Rule allows field work by the monks, Benedict passes from the artisans of the monastery (*RM* 85) to the postulants (*RM* 87-90). In conformity with his model, he is going to give rules, first for the admission of new members of the community and afterwards for the election of a new abbot. The two topics are connected: they both pertain to the monastery's future. Wisely located by the Master near the end of his Rule, they retain this very natural position with Benedict, who nevertheless will add to what forms the final chapter of both Rules ("On the gate and gatekeepers") a series of appendices, plus an epilogue.

The admission of new recruits

The Master's four chapters on the admission of postulants have been reduced by Benedict to a single chapter (*RB* 58) where we again encounter most of the arrangements of the earlier Rule but set forth in a new and more coherent order, with a good number of varied innovations.

One of the most remarkable of these novelties is the creation of a separate house for the newcomers and the task of formation entrusted to "an elder fit to win souls." For the Master the candidates stayed at the guesthouse under the surveillance of two supervisors assigned once a week to watch the guests who spent two months of waiting there before they were admitted to their profession. For Benedict they only stay a few days at the guesthouse, and are then transferred to the "novitiate house" where they stay not just for two months but for an entire year, since two further periods of waiting, of six and four months respectively, have been added to what was required by the Master.

Each of these three periods of probation ends with reading the Rule which the novice must accept with full awareness. This prescribes three times as much as the Master's Rule which spoke over and over again to the novices about reading the Rule (*RM* 87.3; 89.1; 90.5; 90.64) but did not formally distinguish or enumerate the readings.

The whole year (adding up the three periods of two, six and four months) recalls not only the *Institutions* of Cassian but also what the Master had prescribed for the lay postulants: they had to wait one year before they were given a monastic habit and tonsure (*RM* 90). This long period is in contrast with the simple delay of two months required by the Master for "converts", that is, for religious persons living in the world who already bore the character of being consecrated when they asked for admission to the monastery.

Removing the Master's distinction between lay and "convert", Benedict imposes the same period of one year upon all, at the beginning of which he nevertheless inserts the two months his predecessor had required. The same spirit of synthesis leads him to combine the ceremony of profession that ended the Master's two month period, with the ceremony of tonsure and habit that marked the completion of the probationary year. At the heart of the unique act of engagement that the new Rule institutes, we find the Psalm verse *Receive me, Lord, according to your word, and I will live* (Ps. 118, 116). The Master had the newly professed chant this verse, but now it has been tripled and augmented by a *Gloria Patri*, while a second Psalm verse *Confirm, O Lord, what you have ac-*

complished among us (Ps. 67, 29) placed by the Master in the mouth of the abbot, now disappears; in place of the response by the abbot, the newly professed hears his own invocation repeated three times *by the community.*

Moving from one Rule to another, we can take note of a more general change: while the Master began by giving lengthy instructions in utmost detail for the candidate's renunciation of all his possessions and made this material renunciation itself the principal object of the newly-professed monk's declaration, Benedict speaks about renouncing possessions only by way of a parenthetical remark inserted into the ritual of profession. At the same time, he dwells at leisure on other, more spiritual aspects of the commitment. In this connection, we should, at least, emphasize the mission given to the Benedictine master of novices: to watch carefully and make sure that the candidate is "truly seeking God", that is, to see "if he is applying himself with care to the Work of God, to obedience, to the practice of humility." The triple formula of profession has the same intention: the brother "promises perseverance, a regular life, and obedience", without any mention being made of the renunciation of possessions. Now these three objects of the final commitment already appear, one after the other, in the three waiting periods that precede the profession, of which the first and third conclude, respectively, with a promise of perseverance and obedience, while the second, less clearly stated, appears to have regularity of life for its object.

Children, priests, foreign monks

Relegated by Benedict to the background within the great treatise we have just been reviewing, the question of material goods recovers in the following chapter all the emphasis that the Master had given it. The chapters in both Rules on the oblation of children (*RM* 91; *RB* 59) only discuss the measures taken by the parents or the commitment required of them concerning the possessions their son would inherit. In sum, the young oblate cannot have any hope at all of receiving this inheritance since to do so might change his mind completely.

Two other kinds of recruits form the object of the following chapters. First, priests who would like to live in the monastery. Such priests were turned away by the Master (*RM* 83) who received them as temporary guests only; Benedict receives these members of the clergy as long as they submit to the Rule. The priests can even receive a place of honor befitting their sacred functions (*RB* 60).

The second special case is that of monks who have come from other monasteries. In this situation, even Benedict's predecessor was receptive (*RM* 79, 23-28) and Benedict abundantly so, but with several new considerations which makes his version of the matter—strange to say—two or three times longer than that of the Master (*RB* 61).

In the same innovative line, the Benedictine Rule provides for a procedure that is entirely absent from the previous legislation: the ordination of monks to the presbyterate or diaconate (*RB* 62). Benedict's primary concern here is to protect abbatial authority and regular observance from any possible encroachment on the part of a monk who has become a priest. Further, such ordinations pose anew the question of the ranking of the brothers, a question already treated in connection with the secular clerics and monks from other monasteries who have been received into the community. Like these specially honored recruits, the monks who have been ordained as deacons or priests can take a position superior to their entry level. But this level remains their normal position, to which they always can—and are sometimes forced to—return.

Order of the community and mutual relationships

The issue of rank within the monastery which has been touched on several times in the foregoing pages, is the principal subject of a substantial chapter (*RB* 63) which Benedict inserts immediately after the treatment of ordinations. Connected in this way to the section on recruitment, this treatise on the ranking of the brothers is not without reference to the chapter that follows on the "ordination" of the abbot. For the Master, it seems, the procedure for designating a new abbot was an opportunity to enlarge with solemnity on one of his favorite principles: that no fixed order at all ought to be established among the brethren, so as to leave entirely unforeseen the abbot's choice of successor, a choice to be postponed to the last minute before the abbot's death, in order to stimulate in everyone the ambition to attain to the supreme position (*RM* 92).

Wisely rejecting such competition in virtue, Benedict restores the order of seniority that recalls the Pachomian origins of community life. Accordingly, he removes the prohibition of all ranking with which the Master began his treatise on abbatial succession, and replaces it with a chapter entitled "On the Order of the Community" (*RB* 63). In this chapter, without saying a word to call attention to the fact, he takes up precisely the opposite position as his predecessor.

The foundation of the community's order is seniority: each one occupies a place corresponding to the date of his entrance. However, this order of seniority can be modified in consideration of particular merits or by a decision of the abbot. Apart from these two criteria, the monks are ranked according to the time they have spent in the monastery. Spiritual age, as determined by the supernatural rebirth of profession, replaces ordinary age.

After having established order among the brothers, Benedict then indicates the relationships that should obtain among the ranks: the younger should honor the older, the older should love the younger. As for the abbot, they must both honor and love him, for the sake of the Christ whom he represents. We recognize here an echo of the definition with which began the chapter on the abbot as the representative of Christ (*RB* 2). Similarly, when Benedict emphasizes that the natural age of children does not render them in any way inferior to adults, he renews an observation he made before at the beginning of the Rule concerning the counsel of the brothers (*RB* 3). Again, the twin precept of honoring the elder and loving the younger reproduces a pair of sentences from the chapter on "The Instruments of Good Works" (*RB* 4).

The election of the abbot; a second set of guidelines for the abbot

After having re-established the traditional principle of seniority by way of an innovation on the Master, Benedict returns to another general practice that had been laid aside by his predecessor: the election of an abbot by the community (*RB* 64).

In fact, just as the Christian people of a city in antiquity elected their own bishop, just so the monks of each community would choose their abbot, at least in principle. But this normal system of episcopal election suffered an interruption at Rome in the first quarter of the sixth century, owing to serious disorders; to avoid this, each pope was assigned the responsibility to designate his own successor. On this point, as on others, the Master had imitated the great Church in the neighborhood by entrusting to the dying abbot the choice of his own replacement.

This system of "nomination by predecessor" was abrogated at Rome around 530 and was likewise abandoned by

Benedict near the middle of the century. The right of the monks to the choice of their abbot had been recognized by the community of Lerins one hundred years earlier, at a council held at Arles. But at the same time as it restores this ancient custom, the new Rule also changes it in two respects. First, it stipulates that the judgment of an enlightened minority ought to be preferred to the defective choice of a majority, and this presupposes the intervention of superior authority. Second, it specifies that the chosen candidate can and ought to be rejected if he connives at the vicious tendencies of those who elect him. In such circumstances, the bishops and Christian people in the vicinity are invited to overturn an election and "provide the House of God with a worthy administrator."

After he has ruled on the new abbot's promotion to his position, Benedict proceeds to trace out a program of governance that recalls the code of abbatial conduct at the beginning of the Rule. He is now following the Master, but not without some modification. For the present, he edits rather freely, but on many occasions he recalls the counsel given to the superior by Augustine toward the end of the latter's *Praeceptum*. The idea itself (of exhorting the abbot in the final pages of the Rule) may have come to him from Augustine. In any case, he is thinking of Augustine when he recommends the newly elected abbot to "think always of the account he will have to render" to God, to "hate vices and love the brothers", to "strive to be loved more than feared", and to "serve more than rule", which last precept is not in Augustine's Rule but can be found in other writings of the Great Doctor.

While this lovely passage owes almost nothing to the Master, it is perhaps from the latter that the final exhortation comes to "keep the present Rule in all of its points". Indeed, for the Master, the former abbot solemnly handed over the Rule of the monastery to the new abbot in the course of the ceremony of abbatial benediction (*RM* 93, 24-26). It is possible that this rite of handing-down the *Regula,* along with the short speech that accompanies it, had suggested to Benedict that before he concluded his Rule, he should "recommend it" to the abbot.

The provost of the monastery

From the Master as well, doubtless, comes the inspiration for the following chapter (*RB* 65) where Benedict discusses the abbot's second in command, called the "provost" (*praepositus*). We should recall that the Master prohibited all fixed order among the brothers and he especially opposed the nomination of a "second" who might appear as the abbot's future successor. Nevertheless he also provided that the appointment of a second-in-command could be instituted *per accidens.* If a dying abbot who has already named a successor regains his health, he can reassume the government of the community, but he will keep beside him as a second-in-command the one he has designated to succeed. This incidental second-in-command must otherwise show himself in complete submission. If he does not, he will be left aside, and the search for the abbatial succession will begin again. (*RM* 93, 43-90).

Along the lines of his predecessor, Benedict therefore adds another chapter on the provost to his treatment of abbatial succession. He differs from the Master in admitting the nomination of this second-ranking superior, just as he had restored the order of seniority. But he shows much reserve when he comes to the provost's function in which he sees a possible inroad for worse disorders. It is better, he thinks, that the abbot be assisted only by the deans. Since these are multiple, they are not as liable to pride and insubordination as a provost who is the sole member of his classification.

Difficulties between the abbot and the provost are particularly to be feared when both superiors have been instituted together by the same bishop and the same abbots. Benedict vehemently opposes such a simultaneous installation of two chiefs. It is the abbot, and he alone, who ought to nominate his provost, along with all the officers of the monastery. And yet, despite this diatribe by Benedict against the simultaneous nomination of the superior and his deputy by the same external authorities, Gregory reports the curious fact that for the foundation at Terracine, the abbot of Monte Cassino acted as follows: he himself nominated, together at one time, both the "Father" of the new monastery *and* the "Second" (*Dialogues* II, 22.1)!

As the Master, so Benedict concludes by foreseeing what errors the provost would have to commit for him to be removed by the abbot. Going farther than the earlier Rule, the new Rule even provides for the expulsion of a culpable provost. We are concerned precisely here with the crimes of pride. Nevertheless, the abbot, on his part, can yield to another vice to which Benedict alerts him: jealousy. The Master never envisaged that the one who represents Christ in the monastery could succumb to this temptation! Such realistic understanding of the weaknesses of the abbot is one of the novelties of the Benedictine Rule.

Chapter Nine

Conclusion, Appendices, Epilogue

In its original form, the Rule of Benedict, like that of the Master, came to an end with the chapter on the gatekeepers or porters (*RM* 95, *RB* 66). The gate and the enclosure of the monastery are fitting themes for a conclusion! Furthermore, Benedict completed the chapter by prescribing frequent community reading of the Rule. Augustine had ended with an analogous regulation: the Rule had to be re-read once per week. The phrasing of Benedict has the sound of a conclusion, confirming the suspicion that the Rule ended here in its first edition.

From now on, the chapters have the appearance of *additions*. The first of these supplements was perhaps the epilogue (*RB* 73) the first phrase of which begins with the same words — *Regulam autem hanc* — as the end of the chapter on the gatekeepers (*Hanc autem regulam*). But in between a total of six small chapters seems to have been inserted (*RB* 67-72). The interest of these appendices is considerable: we see affirmed in them especially the concern for fraternal relations, a theme to which the Master paid so little attention.

The gate and the taking of journeys outside the monastery

The preoccupation with interpersonal relationships that is so peculiar to Benedict extends all the way to the chapter on the gatekeepers (or "porters") a chapter that is nevertheless common to both authors. Following his custom, the Master traced out precise regulations for the two gatekeepers, assigning them a definite location and well defined tasks, without forgetting the table at which they take their meals. Like his predecessor, Benedict wants to have them live near the gate but this proximity is justified by him with reasons lacking in the Master: it is necessary that the visitors "find him always present to respond to them. And as soon as anyone knocks or if a pauper calls, he is to reply, 'Thanks be to God' (*Deo Gratias*) or ask for a blessing (*Benedic*) and with all the sweetness of the fear of God he will hasten to respond with the fervor of charity". In a new way the Benedictine Rule brings into the light the main obligation, really the unique one, of this position which is to welcome all those who arrive at the gate in a Christian manner, with faith and love.

Also like the Master, Benedict requires that "everything necessary" for material life be available on the inside of the monastic enclosure with the intention of avoiding as much as possible any journeys outside, with all their inconveniences. And he is in accord with his predecessor as well in prescribing to the brothers the frequent reading of the Rule. But whereas the Master regulated the reading of one of the chapters to be made in the refectory daily during the meal, Benedict does not specify where or when the "frequent" reading of the Rule is to take place. His concluding phrase, so formulated, is still more vague than that of Augustine who prescribed the "reading of this little book once per week".

The first chapter that Benedict adds to the one on the gatekeepers very naturally concerns the outside journeyings and returnings of the brothers who have been sent outside (*RB* 67). This question which was treated by the Master in chapters that came much sooner than his own chapter on gatekeepers (*RM* 66-67) appears in Benedict with several new precisions. The most important of these regards the reason why the monks who re-enter the monastery are to ask for prayers from their brothers: there is fear lest "they have allowed themselves to see some evil thing or hear some careless word on their journey" (*cf.* Matt. 12, 36).

Obedience in impossible things

At first sight, the appendix that follows this (*RB* 68) seems to be without any relation to what precedes it: treating "impossible commands", it appears to begin a new subject with nothing that could tie it in with the instructions about the gatekeepers or journeys outside the monastery. However, an earlier passage of the Master (*RM* 57, 14-16) shows that brothers who had been sent outside would sometimes rebel against the commands of their mission, no doubt because their trips entailed much effort and sacrifice. This may have been the association of ideas that connects the journeys just treated and the "impossible commands" that Benedict is now considering.

Whatever its relationship to the preceding, this little chapter is clearly inspired by the Basilian Rule and the Pseudo-Basilian *Admonition to a Spiritual Son*. Just as these sources had done, the Benedictine Rule invites a brother who feels thus overwhelmed to explain the difficulties to his superior. But in addition the Rule prescribes accepting the order beforehand "in all sweetness and obedience", and after his making his explanation to the superior, he is to obey with faith, hope and love if the command is still insisted upon. The explanation should be made "patiently and at an opportune moment, without pride, resistance, or contradiction".

Basil had only touched on the topic lightly, but the matter is here treated in a complete way, with each of its three phases allowing room for perfectly clear spiritual direction. The whole is a masterpiece, and only the wonderful chapter on "good zeal" (*RB* 72) is comparable to it.

Who may protect or punish?

We find Basil once again in the background of the next chapter, but it is above all the Pachomian Rule that stands behind this piece and its complement where Benedict prohibits, in turn, first (*RB* 69) the "defense" of a member of the community who seems to have been treated unjustly and then (*RB* 70) the striking or excommunication of anyone without the command of the abbot. Ignored by the Master, these two opposed behaviors both belong to the realm of interpersonal relationships to which Benedict is particularly attentive in these appendices.

Mutual obedience

The concern for fraternal relationships shows itself again in the chapter entitled, "That they should mutually obey one another" (*RB* 71). Here Benedict refers to two principles of which one is the Master's, the other his own: the "good of obedience" enshrined by the earlier Rule and the principle of rank by seniority which the new Rule has been establishing.

"Obedience is the path by which we reach God"; consequently it must be profitable to obey not only the abbot and the officers he has appointed, but even the other members of the community. In this expansion of obedience which is not only hierarchical but also mutual, the "good" that one derives from it no longer consists in the direction one receives from a representative of Christ, duly instructed by Him to make His will known, but rather consists in the *imitation* of Christ, obedient to His Father unto death. The teaching "He who hears you, hears me" (Luke 10, 16) is less significant here than that other statement of Jesus: "I did not come here to do my own will, but the will of Him Who sent me" (John 6, 38).

Nevertheless, this "mutual" obedience retains something of a hierarchical nature: in practice, Benedict specifies that each will obey his "elders". The reciprocal of this is not envisaged: nobody owes obedience to the younger. It is only in the next chapter, on "good zeal" that obedience will become mutual without restriction.

The same limitation is to be observed in the second half of the present chapter where Benedict instructs the younger monks to accept humbly the reprimands of their elders. Commands and reprimands all go in the same direction, from high to low. Moreover, whatever comes from above has to be received below under pain of sanction. These penal statements accentuate the juridical and narrowly disciplinarian aspect of this section, but they must be supplemented by the spiritual note introduced by the lawgiver when he exhorts the monks to obey "in total charity and eagerness". We find here the motif of love which Benedict never fails to associate with the precept of obedience, in season and out.

The manifestations of good zeal

Describing next the "good zeal which the monks ought to have" (*RB* 72) Benedict is able to recall the "zeal for the good" that the Master hoped to maintain among the monks by setting up "a competition in virtue" for the goal of being chosen as abbot. But several of the traits of zeal that he enumerates lead us to think especially of his own chapters on the order of the community and on mutual obedience. Having already established the order of seniority and the quasi-hierarchical relations between young and old, he transcends this order now by advocating purely and simply, "mutual honor" and "rivaling one another in obedience", without making the least mention of rank.

This justly celebrated chapter deserves to be reproduced here in full:

> As there is an evil zeal and love that separates us from God and leads us to hell, just so there is a good zeal that separates us from our vices and leads to God and eternal life. This, then, is the zeal the monks must practice with a burning love, "outdoing each other in showing honor" (Romans 12, 10); let them put up with each others' corporal and moral infirmities without any impatience; let them compete in showing each other obedience; let nobody seek out what is to his own advantage, but what is to the advantage of the other; let them practice fraternal charity with disinterestedness; let them fear God with love; let them show affection to their abbot with a sincere and humble charity, and let them prefer absolutely nothing to Christ [Cyprian, Or. 15]. May He lead us all to eternal life!

Of these eight signs of good zeal, the first five have to do with inter-fraternal relationships while the last three have to do with God, the abbot, and Christ. Since the abbot represents Christ, one could say that the first five effects of zeal refer to the love of neighbor while the last three refer to the love of God. The naming of Christ at the end permits the chapter to end with the desire of reaching (*perducat*) eternal life which echoes the end of the chapter's first sentence: "… good zeal … leads to (*ducit ad*) God and eternal life".

This transcendence of inequalities that exist among the monks by their seniority ranking leads us to think of the elimination of differences between Christians that baptism brings. According to Saint Paul, among Christians "there is no longer slave or free, neither male nor female". But the suppression of such categories remains in the mystical order, because slave and free, man and woman remain what they are, after baptism as before, and Pauline ethics is based on these differences. In an analogous fashion, the chapter on good zeal abstracts from the marks that distinguish the monks—young and old—and transcends them in a rising surge of charity without, however, suppressing or abrogating what has been said about the hierarchical relationships they are to maintain among themselves, founded on seniority.

The epilogue

Benedict's epilogue (*RB* 73)—in the first version it may have followed immediately after the chapter on the gatekeepers (*RB* 66)—recalls the prologue at the beginning and end of which the meaning of the entire enterprise was indicated. Both "extremities" of the prologue, then, are directed to the individual reader, addressed as "you". The same address to the second person singular reappears in the last phrase of the epilogue.

The tone of the epilogue is very modest. The Rule, which is now completed, does not attempt to lead to perfection but only furnishes the point of departure for those who wish to attain to perfection. To go beyond the rudiments it proposes, it is necessary to have recourse to the Sacred Scriptures, the writings of the Catholic Fathers, the works of Cassian (*Conferences* and *Institutions*) of Saint Basil (*Rule*) as well as the *Lives of the Fathers*. This last title certainly designates above all the systematic collection of apothegms already cited formally by Benedict on two occasions, when discussing the recitation of the Psalms (*RB* 18) and abstention from wine (*RB* 40); both references included the same sense of the decadence of contemporary monasticism when compared to those ancient mountain-peaks of virtue.

This feeling of a deplorable gap between "the Fathers and us" differentiates Benedict from the Master for whom the example of the Fathers does not represent an almost unattainable ideal and a kind of permanent reproach but a model to which one can and ought to conform oneself in the present time by observing the Rule.

> You then, whoever you are, who are hurrying toward your heavenly homeland, carry out with the help of Christ this little Rule for beginners which we have now finished. In that way alone will you reach with God's protection, the most elevated summits of doctrine and virtue we have been speaking about. Amen.

"You will reach" (*pervenies*). This is the last word of Benedict's epilogue and it recalls the expression "reach our Creator" (*perveniamus ad Creatorem nostrum*) employed a few lines before, *a propos* the books of the Holy Catholic Fathers. And these in their way recall the image of "a return to God", presented at the beginning of the prologue. These metaphors of the journey and the racetrack speak well of the unique design of the whole work which is to lead each monk to encounter, in Christ, the vision of his Creator.

Postscript

Saint Benedict Today

At the end of this little book, the time seems right to cast a glance over the posterity of St. Benedict and the legacy of his work in our day. The hand of cards we have been dealt today is not without its trumps, to allow us to play well and seriously the game of the monastic life according to the example of Benedict and according to his Rule. The recent development of research in ancient monasticism permits us to situate the figure of the Saint and his legislation more precisely in their historical context, while the new freedoms offered by the post-conciliar *aggiornamento* makes possible rediscoveries and renaissances in several domains.

The element of the miraculous which fills the biography of Benedict need not prevent the reader of the third millennium from following attentively the spiritual progress sketched out by Gregory the Great. The four temptations Gregory has his hero undergo during the Subiaco period allow us to observe a complete purification of the soul, corrected by stages in each of its three major components: the rational faculty, menaced by vainglory; the concupiscible appetite, leading to sexual desire; the irascible appetite, source of anger and hatred. When the third of these had been tested two times, the monk of Subiaco could claim to be perfectly master of himself in the eyes of God, and henceforth fit for the charismatic influence that he would be continually exercising at Monte Cassino, until his sister, more loving and more potent than he, would set a term to his great deeds and cause him to enter upon visions of the world to come.

In addition to this progressive purification which is still the central program in the life of every monk — and really in the life of every Christian — the second book of the *Dialogues* shows us a tension between two ways of being a monk: that of the cenobite, or one who lives in community, and that of the hermit. In paradoxical way, Benedict begins with the latter, but his three years of solitary life in the grotto are in a kind of hidden symbiosis with the community of Romanus and Adeodatus. And then again, after the check on his first pridefulness, he returns to his "much-beloved solitude" where he "dwells with himself, alone under the eyes of Him Who looks down from on high". Later, at Monte Cassino, we will see him as abbot pass the night alone in a tower as he keeps his private vigil before leading the community office of prayer. In a passage from the next book of the *Dialogues* (III, 16) Gregory informs us that Benedict was in communication with a certain hermit and recluse on Mount Marsique; Benedict convinced this man to untie himself from the chain that was holding him to the rock.

Turning to the Benedictine Rule, one of the realities permitting us to approach it more closely today is the disassociation of clericalism from monasticism. The latter can now be cultivated for its own sake as in the time of Benedict. For one thing, concelebration happily simplifies the Eucharistic practice of the monasteries. In the same vein, it is not impossible to imagine a return to norm of the sixth-century Italy, evidenced by the Rule of the Master and those of Paul and Stephen just before and just after St. Benedict's time: a simple communion service during the week, before dinner, with the Mass being reserved for Sunday. This sensible system, in harmony with the usages of the Church in the first centuries, would assure to the monks the "daily bread" of the Eucharist, while keeping the greatest emphasis on the Mass and the Lord's Day.

In the domain of community prayer, Benedict's two fundamental principles ought to be preserved with care. The first is the celebration of the seven offices during the day, in addition to the nightly vigils. In this connection, the widespread abandonment of Prime has been a mistake. Judged too superficially as a redundancy, this office of the sunrise is in reality full of meaning, above all in countries where dawn is prolonged; and we now understand that Benedict's intention was to enhance the office with the recitation of psalms that change daily.

Benedict's other norm in this area is the recitation of the entire Psalter each week. Without placing more importance on the precise distribution of the psalms than he did himself, we can be allowed some regret that anarchy has expanded in this area. Happy those who have the wisdom to follow the order of Psalm recitation set down in the Rule! — or who at least observe the weekly recitation of the hundred and fifty Psalms as he desired.

In what concerns physical sustenance, the contemporary practice of monasteries is in opposition to what Benedict prescribes. He, in conformity with the usage of all ancient monasticism, foresaw ordinarily only one meal during the day, or two at the most. Our three daily meals, maintained without variation throughout the year, are a negation of the law of fasting, to which our Fathers attached so much importance. The belief that modern man is too weak to fast like the ancients is a pure myth that no one should take seriously. In a Church which has strangely lost all vestige of the great Biblical and Christian observance of fasting, monks would render a true service to their brothers and sisters by witnessing to the possibility of this practice and its advantages, a practice so intimately bound up with their own monastic tradition.

Other gaps between the Rule and ourselves are to be judged in a more nuanced fashion. For example, the common dormitory provided by Benedict is not an original institution of community life but a custom introduced toward the end of the fifth century in response to certain abuses. By moving to living in individual cells, the monks of the Middle Ages and modern times have returned, consciously or unconsciously, to the primitive usage, attested by the Rule of Pachomius, the *Institutions* of Cassian and other ancient texts. Why not think here of the veneration that Benedict professed for these "Fathers" of the monastic life, for which he wrote his Rule as a kind of introduction?

The Rule of Basil has nothing to advise us on this option for cells or common dormitory. But there is another point on which that Rule, so treasured by Benedict, uniquely clarifies Benedict's own: the question of the monk's habit. In contrast with Evagrius and Cassian, who are content to interpret in symbolical fashion each piece of monastic garb without supplying the profound meaning and *raison d' etre* of the clothing as such, Basil points out its fundamental characteristics: it is *distinctive*, in order to signify the separation from the world; and it must be *uniform*, to show the communion of those who wear it. These two general norms are suited to direct the monks to the solution of the important and delicate problem of their habit. Being faithful in this regard to the Benedictine Rule does not consist in getting dressed for certain ceremonies in the items of clothing mentioned by the Rule, while wearing modern and secular clothes the rest of the time. The essence of monasticism is simplicity, and nothing is more contrary to it than such duplicity.

We could spend some time dealing with some other behaviors of today's monks that likewise do not well accord with the tradition of which Benedict is at once the inheritor and the instrument of propagation. I am thinking particularly of the use of speech which has been vitiated by idle nonsense and pastimes. Such foibles, which exist in all eras, need not prevent us today from thanking God for all that has come down to us, by way of the Benedictine Rule, from the monastic sanctity of the first centuries. The total consecration of chastity, continuous attention to God in loving awe; humble, obedient and patient imitation of Christ—it is enough just to mention these things to catch a glimpse of the magnificent gifts that have come to us from Benedict and his Rule. And when we add to that the complete divestation of property, blessed poverty, and the relationship with Christ, both by way of the superiors (who represent Him) and by way of the fraternal communion after the image of the first Christians—a value Benedict owes especially to St. Augustine—it becomes clear that this Saint (whose life and work this little book has attempted to reveal) remains today, as he has always been, a conspicuous instrument of the Divine Love.

Further Reading

Historical Background:

Brown, Peter, *The Rise of Western Christendom*, Second Edition, Oxford, 2003.

Herrin, Judith, *The Formation of Christendom*, Princeton, 1989.

Markus, R. A. *Gregory the Great and His World*, Cambridge, 1997.

Peterson, Joan M., *The* Dialogues *of Gregory the Great in their Late Antique Cultural Background,* Pontifical Institute of Medieval Studies, Studies and Texts 69, Toronto, Ontario, Canada, 1984.

Primary Sources:

Kardong, Terrence, O.S.B. *Benedict's Rule: A Translation and Commentary,* Collegeville, MN, 1996.

Meisel, Anthony C., and del Mastro, M.L., *The Rule of St. Benedict,* New York, 1975.

Zimmermann, O.J., *Dialogues of Gregory the Great*, Fathers of the Church Series 39, New York, 1959.

Vogüé, Adalbert de, (ed.), La Règle de Saint Benoît, Sources Chrétiennes, 181–186, Paris, 1971–1972.

Vogüé, Adalbert de, (ed.), *Grégoire le Grand: Les Dialogues,* Sources Chrétiennes 251, 260, 265, Paris, 1978.

Vogüé, Adalbert de, (ed.), *La Règle du Maître,* Sources Chretiennes 105–106, Paris, 1964.

Selected Related Works by Adalbert de Vogüé:

Études sur la Règle de saint Benoît. Nouveau recueil (collection Vie Monastique no. 34) Bellefontaine, 1996.

Le monachisme en Occident avant saint Benoît (collection Vie Monastique, no. 35) Bellefontaine, 1998.